THE POETRY & PROSE OF CHARLES BAUDELAIRE

Translated into English with Commentary by

A. S. KLINE

POETRY IN TRANSLATION

www.poetryintranslation.com

© Copyright 2001-2010 A. S. Kline

Cover design by Poetry in Translation

Digital scans or photographs of the images in the main text have been released into
the public domain by various institutions. Identifications and attributions are
provided beneath each image. All related image rights are at the discretion of the
copyright holders of the original images and/or the referenced institutions.

All rights reserved under International and Pan American Copyright Conventions.
Textual content of this work may be freely reproduced, stored and transmitted,
electronically or otherwise, for any non-commercial purpose. Restrictions apply to
adaptation of the work. Usage of any material for commercial purposes resulting in
direct, indirect or incidental commercial gain requires permission to be sought and
granted in writing from the copyright holder. Refer to the Poetry in Translation
copyright statement (*www.poetryintranslation.com/Admin/Copyright.htm*)

Any statements or opinions expressed in this book reflect the views of the author
alone. Although the author has made every effort to ensure that the information in
this book was correct at the time of going to press, the author does not assume and
hereby disclaims any liability to any party for any loss, damage, or disruption caused
by errors or omissions, whether such errors or omissions result from negligence,
accident, or any other cause

Please direct sales or editorial enquiries to:
tonykline@poetryintranslation.com

This print edition is published by
Poetry In Translation (*www.poetryintranslation.com*),
via On-Demand Publishing LLC, (a Delaware limited liability Company that does
business under the name "CreateSpace") in partnership with
Amazon Services UK Limited (a UK limited company with registration number
03223028 and its registered office at 60 Holborn Viaduct, London, Greater
London, EC1A 2BN, UK)

ISBN-10: 1522854363
ISBN-13: 978-1522854364

CONTENTS

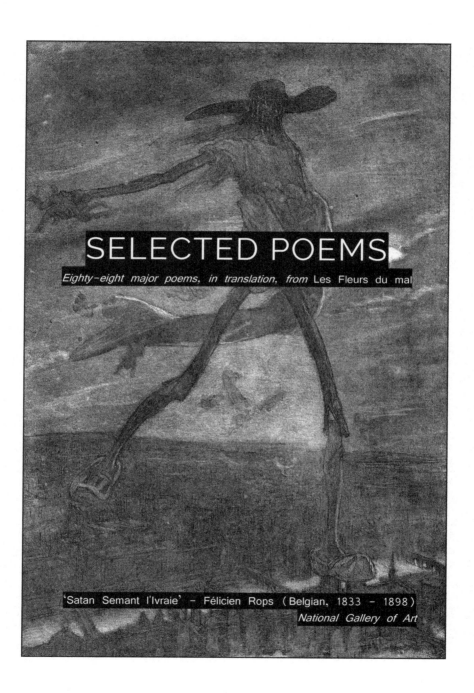

SELECTED POEMS

Eighty-eight major poems, in translation, from Les Fleurs du mal

'Satan Semant l'Ivraie' – Félicien Rops (Belgian, 1833 – 1898)
National Gallery of Art

'N'EST CE PAS QU'IL EST DOUX'

Is it not pleasant, now we are tired,

and tarnished, like other men, to search for those fires

in the furthest East, where, again, we might see

morning's new dawn, and, in mad history,

hear the echoes, that vanish behind us, the sighs

of the young loves, God gives, at the start of our lives?

'IL AIMAIT A LA VOIR'

It was in her white skirts that he loved to see
her run straight through the branches and leaves, gracefully,
but still gauche, and hiding her leg from the light,
when she tore her dress, on the briars, in her flight.

INCOMPATIBILITY

Higher there, higher, far from the ways,
from the farms and the valleys, beyond the trees,
beyond the hills and the grasses' haze,
far from the herd-trampled tapestries,

you discover a sombre pool in the deep
that a few bare snow-covered mountains form.
The lake, in light's, and night's sublime sleep,
is never disturbed in its silent storm.

In that mournful waste, to the unsure ear,
come faint drawn-out sounds, more dead than the bell,
of some far-off cow, the echoes unclear,
as it grazes the slope, of a distant dell.

On those hills where the wind effaces all signs,
on those glaciers, fired by the sun's pure light,
on those rocks, where dizziness threatens the mind,
in that lake's vermilion presage of night,

under my feet, and above my head,

silence, that makes you wish to escape;

that eternal silence, of the mountainous bed

of motionless air, where everything waits.

You would say that the sky, in its loneliness,

gazed at itself in the glass, and, up there,

the mountains listened, in grave watchfulness

to the mystery nothing that's human can hear.

And when, by chance, a wandering cloud

darkens the silent lake, moving by,

you might think that you saw some spirit's robe,

or else its clear shadow, travelling, over the sky.

TO A CREOLE LADY

In a perfumed land caressed by the sun
I found, beneath the trees' crimson canopy,
palms from which languor pours on one's
eyes, the veiled charms of a Creole lady.

Her hue pale, but warm, a dark-haired enchantress,
she shows in her neck's poise the noblest of manners:
slender and tall, she strides by like a huntress,
tranquil her smile, her eyes full of assurance.

If you travelled, my Lady, to the land of true glory,
the banks of the Seine or green Loire, a Beauty
worthy of gracing the manors of olden days,

you'd inspire, among arbours' shadowy secrets,
a thousand sonnets in the hearts of the poets,
whom, more than your blacks, your vast eyes would enslave.

TO A WOMAN OF MALABAR

Your feet are as slender as hands, your hips, to me,
wide enough for the sweetest white girl's envy:
to the wise artist your body is sweet and dear,
and your great velvet eyes black without peer.
In the hot blue lands where God gave you your nature
your task is to light a pipe for your master,
to fill up the vessels with cool fragrance
and chase the mosquitoes away when they dance,
and when dawn sings in the plane-trees, afar,
fetch bananas and pineapples from the bazaar.
All day your bare feet go where they wish
as you hum old lost melodies under your breath,
and when evening's red cloak descends overhead
you lie down sweetly on a straw bed,
where humming birds fill your floating dreams,
as graceful and flowery as you it seems.

Happy child, why do you long to see France

our suffering, and over-crowded land,

and trusting your life to the sailors, your friends,

say a fond goodbye to your dear tamarinds?

Scantily dressed, in muslins, frail,

shivering under the snow and hail,

how you'd pine for your leisure, sweet and free,

body pinned in a corset's brutality,

if you'd to glean supper amongst our vile harms,

selling the scent of exotic charms,

sad pensive eyes searching our fog-bound sleaze,

for the lost ghosts of your coconut-trees!

THE ALBATROSS

Often, for their amusement, bored sailors
take albatrosses, vast sea-birds, that sleep
in the air, indolent fellow travellers,
following the ship skimming the deep.

No sooner are they set down on the boards,
than those kings of the azure, maladroit, shamefully
let their vast white wings, like oars,
trail along their sides, piteously.

Winged traveller, gauche, gross, useless, laughable,
now, one of them, with a pipe stem, prods you,
who, a moment ago, were beautiful:
another, limping, mimics the cripple who flew.

The Poet bears a likeness to that prince of the air,
who mocks at slingshots, and haunts the winds:
on earth, an exile among the scornful, where
he is hampered, in walking, by his giant wings.

BERTHA'S EYES

You can scorn more illustrious eyes,
sweet eyes of my child, through which there takes flight
something as good or as tender as night.
Turn to mine your charmed shadows, sweet eyes!

Great eyes of a child, adorable secrets,
you resemble those grottoes of magic
where, behind the dark and lethargic,
shine vague treasures the world forgets.

My child has veiled eyes, profound and vast,
and shining like you, Night, immense, above!
Their fires are of Trust, mixed with thoughts of Love,
that glitter in depths, voluptuous or chaste.

'JE N'AI PAS OUBLIE, VOISINE DE LA VILLE,'

I've not forgotten, near to the town,

our white house, small but alone:

its Pomona of plaster, its Venus of old

hiding nude limbs in the meagre grove,

and the sun, superb, at evening, streaming,

behind the glass, where its sheaves were bursting,

a huge eye in a curious heaven, present

to gaze at our meal, lengthy and silent,

spreading its beautiful candle glimmer

on the frugal cloth and the rough curtain.

'LA SERVANTE AU GRAND CŒUR
DONT VOUS ETIEZ JALOUSE,'

The great-hearted servant of whom you were jealous,

sleeping her sleep in the humble grass,

shouldn't we take her a few flowers?

The dead, the poor dead, have grief like ours,

and when October sighs, clipper of trees,

round their marble tombs, with its mournful breeze,

they must find the living, ungratefully, wed,

snug in sleep, to the warmth of their bed,

while they, devoured by dark reflection,

without bedfellow, or sweet conversation,

old skeletons riddled with worms, deep frozen,

feel the winter snows trickling round them,

and the years flow by without kin or friend

to replace the wreaths at their railing's end.

If some night, when the logs whistle and flare,

seeing her sitting calm, in that chair,

if on a December night, cold and blue,

I might find her there placed in the room,

solemn, and come from her bed, eternal,

to guard the grown child with her eye, maternal,

what could I answer that pious spirit,

seeing tears under her hollow eyelid?

LANDSCAPE

In order to write my chaste verses I'll lie
like an astrologer near to the sky
and, by the bell-towers, listen in dream
to their solemn hymns on the air-stream.
Hands on chin, from my attic's height
I'll see the workshops of song and light,
the gutters, the belfries those masts of the city,
the vast skies that yield dreams of eternity

It is sweet to see stars being born in the blue,
through the mists, the lamps at the windows, too,
the rivers of smoke climbing the firmament,
and the moon pouring out her pale enchantment.
I'll see the springs, summers, autumns' glow,
and when winter brings the monotonous snow
I'll close all my doors and shutters tight
and build palaces of faery in the night.
Then I'll dream of blue-wet horizons,
weeping fountains of alabaster, gardens,
kisses, birdsong at morning or twilight,
all in the Idyll that is most childlike.

The mob that are beating in vain on the glass,

won't make me raise my head as they pass.

Since I'll be plunged deep in the thrill

of evoking the springtime through my own will,

raising the sun out of my own heart,

making sweet air from my burning thought.

THE SUN

Through the streets where at windows of old houses
the persian blinds hide secret luxuries,
when the cruel sun strikes with redoubled fury
on the roofs and fields, the meadows and city,
I go alone in my crazy sword-play
scenting a chance rhyme on every road-way,
stumbling on words and over the pavement
finding verses I often dreamed might be sent.

This nurturing father, anaemia's foe
stirs, in the fields, the worm and the rose,
makes our cares evaporate into the blue,
fills the hives and our brains with honey-dew.
It is he who gives youth to the old man, the cripple,
makes them like young girls, happy and gentle,
and commands the crops to grow ripe in an hour
of the immortal heart, that so longs to flower.

When he shines on the town, a poet that sings,

he redeems the fate of the meanest things,

like a king he enters, no servants, alone,

all palaces, all hospitals where men moan.

SORROWS OF THE MOON

The moon dreams more languidly this evening:
like a sweet woman, in the pillows, at rest,
with her light hand, discretely stroking,
before she sleeps, the curve of her breast,

dying, she gives herself to deep trance,
and casts her eyes over snow-white bowers,
on the satined slope of a soft avalanche,
rising up into the blue, like flowers.

When she sometimes lets fall a furtive tear,
in her secret languor, on our world here,
a pious poet, enemy of sleep's art,

takes that pale tear in the hollow of his palm,
its rainbow glitter like an opal shard,
and far from the sun sets it in his heart.

DON JUAN IN HELL

When Don Juan went down to Hell's charms,

and paid Charon his obol's fare,

he, a sombre beggar with Antisthenes' glare,

gripped the oars with strong avenging arms.

Showing their sagging breasts through open robes

the women writhed under the black firmament

and, like a crowd of sacred victims, broke

behind him into long incessant lament.

Sganarelle laughing demanded his score,

while Don Luis, with trembling hand,

showed the wandering dead, along the shore,

the insolent son who spurned his command.

By the treacherous spouse, who was her lover,

chaste, skinny Elvira shivered in mourning dress,

seeming to ask a last smile of him, where

there might shine his first vow's tenderness.

Gripping the helm cutting the black wave,

erect in armour, stood a giant of stone,

but the hero, leaning, quiet, on his sword-blade,

scornful of all things, gazed at the sea's foam.

ON TASSO IN PRISON
(EUGÈNE DELACROIX'S PAINTING)

The poet in his cell, unkempt and sick,

who crushes underfoot a manuscript,

measures, with a gaze that horror has inflamed,

the stair of madness where his soul was maimed.

The intoxicating laughter that fills his prison

with the absurd and the strange, swamps his reason.

Doubt surrounds him, and ridiculous fear,

hideous and multiform, circles near.

That genius pent up in a foul sty,

those spectres, those grimaces, the cries,

whirling, in a swarm, about his hair,

that dreamer, whom his lodging's terrors bare,

such are your emblems, Soul, singer of songs obscure,

whom Reality suffocates behind four walls!

FEMMES DAMNÉES

Like pensive cattle, lying on the sands,
they turn their eyes towards the sea's far hills,
and, feet searching each other's, touching hands,
know sweet languor and the bitterest thrills.

Some, where the stream babbles, deep in the woods,
their hearts enamoured of long intimacies,
go spelling out the loves of their own girlhoods,
and carving the green bark of young trees.

Others, like Sisters, walk, gravely and slow,
among the rocks, full of apparitions,
where Saint Anthony saw, like lava flows,
the bared crimson breasts of his temptations.

There are those, in the melting candle's glimmer,
who in mute hollows of caves still pagan,
call on you to relieve their groaning fever,
O Bacchus, to soothe the remorse of the ancients!

And others, whose throats love scapularies,

who, hiding whips under their long vestment,

in the sombre groves of the night, solitaries,

blend the sweats of joy with the tears of torment.

O virgins, o demons, o monsters, o martyrs,

great spirits, despisers of reality,

now full of cries, now full of tears,

pious and lustful, seeking infinity,

you, whom my soul has pursued to your hell,

poor sisters, I adore you as much as I weep,

for your dismal sufferings, thirsts that swell,

and the vessels of love, where your great hearts steep!

THE LITANIES OF SATAN

O you, the most knowing, and loveliest of Angels,
a god fate betrayed, deprived of praises,

O Satan, take pity on my long misery!

O, Prince of exile to whom wrong has been done,
who, vanquished, always recovers more strongly,

O Satan, take pity on my long misery!

You who know everything, king of the underworld,
the familiar healer of human distress,

O Satan, take pity on my long misery!

You who teach even lepers, accursed pariahs,
through love itself the taste for Paradise,

O Satan, take pity on my long misery!

O you who on Death, your ancient true lover,

engendered Hope – that lunatic charmer!

O Satan, take pity on my long misery!

You who grant the condemned that calm, proud look

that damns a whole people crowding the scaffold,

O Satan, take pity on my long misery!

You who know in what corners of envious countries

a jealous God hid those stones that are precious,

O Satan, take pity on my long misery!

You whose clear eye knows the deep caches

where, buried, the race of metals slumbers,

O Satan, take pity on my long misery!

You whose huge hands hide the precipice,

from the sleepwalker on the sky-scraper's cliff,

O Satan, take pity on my long misery!

You who make magically supple the bones

of the drunkard, out late, who's trampled by horses,

O Satan, take pity on my long misery!

You who taught us to mix saltpetre with sulphur

to console the frail human being who suffers,

O Satan, take pity on my long misery!

You who set your mark, o subtle accomplice,

on the forehead of Croesus, the vile and pitiless,

O Satan, take pity on my long misery!

You who set in the hearts and eyes of young girls

the cult of the wound, adoration of rags,

O Satan, take pity on my long misery!

The exile's staff, the light of invention,

confessor to those to be hanged, to conspirators,

O Satan, take pity on my long misery!

Father, adopting those whom God the Father

drove in dark anger from the earthly paradise,

O Satan, take pity on my long misery!

Note: Croesus was the king of Lydia (c560-546BC), famed for his wealth. He was defeated and captured by Cyrus of Persia at the taking of Sardis, and rescued by his conqueror from the pyre (Herodotus 1.86)

BEAUTY

O mortals, I am beautiful, like a stone dream,
and my breast, where each man has bruised his soul,
is created to inspire in poets a goal
as eternal and mute as matter might seem.

An inscrutable Sphinx, I am throned in blue sky:
I unite the swan's white with a heart of snow:
I hate all movement that ruffles the flow,
and I never cry and I never smile.

The poets, in front of my poses, so grand
they seem borrowed from ancient tomb-covers,
will exhaust their days in studying a hand,

since I, to fascinate my docile lovers,
have pure mirrors that magnify everything's beauty:
my eyes, my huge eyes, bright with eternity.

LETTER TO SAINTE-BEUVE

On the old oak benches, more shiny and polished
than links of a chain that were, each day, burnished
rubbed by our human flesh, we, still un-bearded,
trailed our ennui, hunched, round-shouldered,
under the four-square heaven of solitude,
where a child drinks study's tart ten-year brew.
It was in those days, outstanding and memorable,
when the teachers, forced to loosen our classical
fetters, yet all still hostile to your rhyming,
succumbed to the pressure of our mad duelling,
and allowed a triumphant, mutinous, pupil
to make Triboulet howl in Latin, at will.
Which of us in those days of pale adolescence
didn't share the weary torpor of confinement,
- eyes lost in the dreary blue of a summer sky
or the snowfall's whiteness, we were dazzled by,
ears pricked, eager, waiting – a pack of hounds
drinking some book's far echo, a riot's sound?

Most of all in summer, that melted the leads,

the walls high, blackened, filled with dread,

with the scorching heat, or when autumn haze

lit the sky with its one monotonous blaze

and made the screeching falcons fall asleep,

white pigeons' terrors, in their slender keep:

the season of reverie when the Muse clings

through the endless day to some bell that rings:

when Melancholy at noon when all is drowsing

at the corridor's end, chin in hand, dragging –

eyes bluer and darker than Diderot's Nun,

that sad, obscene tale known to everyone,

– her feet weighed down by premature ennui,

her brow from night's moist languor un-free.

– and unhealthy evenings, then, feverish nights,

that make young girls love their bodies outright,

and, sterile pleasure, gaze in their mirrors to see

the ripening fruits of their own nubility: –

Italian evenings of thoughtless lethargy,

when knowledge of false delights is revealed

when sombre Venus, on her high black balcony,

out of cool censers, waves of musk sets free.

In this war of enervating circumstances,

matured by your sonnets, prepared by your stanzas,

one evening, having sensed the soul of your art,

I transported Amaury's story into my heart.

Every mystical void is but two steps away

from doubt. – The potion, drop by drop, day by day,

filtering through me, I, drawn to the abyss since I

was fifteen, who swiftly deciphered René's sigh,

I parched by some strange thirst for the unknown,

within the smallest of arteries, made its home.

I absorbed it all, the perfumes, the miasmas,

the long-vanished memories' sweetest whispers,

the drawn-out tangle of phrases, their symbols,

the rosaries murmuring in mystical madrigals,

– a voluptuous book, if ever one was brewed.

Now, whether I'm deep in some leafy refuge,

or in the sun of a second hemispheres' days,

the eternal swell swaying the ocean waves,

the view of endless horizons always re-born,

draw my heart to the dream divine, once more,

be it in heavy languor of burning summer,

or shivering idleness of early December,

beneath tobacco-smoke clouds, hiding the ceiling,

through the book's subtle mystery, always leafing,

a book so dear to those numb souls whose destiny

has, one and all, stamped them with that same malady,

in front of the mirror, I've perfected the cruelty

of the art that, at birth, some demon granted me,

— art of that pain that creates true voluptuousness, —

scratching the wound, to draw blood from my distress.

Poet, is it an insult, or a well-turned compliment?

For regarding you I'm like a lover, to all intent,

faced with a ghost whose gestures are caresses,

with hand, eye of unknown charms, who blesses,

in order to drain one's strength. — All loved beings

are cups of venom one drinks with eyes unseeing,

and the heart that's once transfixed, seduced by pain,

finds death, while still blessing the arrow, every day.

Notes: Baudelaire in 1844 sent this poem to Saint-Beuve, whose novel *Volupté* has Amaury as its hero. Triboulet (c1479-1536), was the court jester of Louis XII, and Francois 1st, who inspired a scene in Rabelais' *Gargantua and Pantagruel*. Diderot was the author of *La Religieuse*, Chateaubriand of *René*.

ELEVATION

High over the ponds, high over the vales,
the mountains, clouds, woods and meres,
beyond the sun, beyond the ethereal veils,
beyond the confines of the starry spheres,

you ride, my spirit, ride with agility,
swooning with joy, at the wave, strong swimmer
and take your ineffable masculine pleasure,
cutting through that endless immensity.

Fly far away from this deathly miasma:
go, purify yourself in the upper air,
and drink like a pure and divine liquor,
what fills limpid space, that lucid fire.

Behind him the boredoms, the vast distress,
that imposes its weight on fog-bound beings,
happy the man, who on vigorous wings
mounts towards fields, serene and luminous!

He whose thoughts, like larks, go soaring,

flying freely towards dawn air, -

who glides above life: grasps, easily, there,

the language of flowers and silent Things!

CORRESPONDENCES

Nature is a temple, where, from living pillars, a flux
of confused words is, sometimes, allowed to fall:
Man travels it, through forests of symbols, that all
observe him, with familiar looks.

Like far echoes that distantly congregate,

in a shadowy and profound unity,

vast as the night air, in its clarity,

perfumes, colours, sounds reverberate.

There are fresh perfumes, like the flesh of children,

mellow as oboes, green as prairies,

- and others, rich, glorious and forbidden,

having the expansive power of infinities,

amber, musk, benjamin and incense,

that sing of the ecstasies of spirit and sense.

THE JEWELS

My sweetheart was naked, knowing my desire,

she wore only her tinkling jewellery,

whose splendour yields her the rich conquering fire

of Moorish slave-girls in the days of their beauty.

When, dancing, it gives out its sharp sound of mockery,

that glistening world of metal and stone,

I am ravished by ecstasy, love like fury

those things where light mingles with sound.

So she lay there, let herself be loved,

and, from the tall bed, she smiled with delight

on my love deep and sweet as the sea is moved,

rising to her as toward a cliff's height.

Like a tamed tigress, her eyes fixed on me

with a vague dreamy air, she tried out her poses,

so wantonly and so innocently,

it gave a new charm to her metamorphoses:

and her arm and her leg, and her back and her thigh,

shining like oil, undulating like a swan's,

passed in front of my calm, clairvoyant eye:

and her belly and breasts, those vine-clustered ones,

thrust out, more seductively than Angels of evil,

to trouble the repose where my soul had its throne,

and topple it from the crystal hill,

where it was seated, calm and alone.

I thought I saw Antiope's hips placed

on a youth's bust, with a new design's grace,

her pelvis accentuated so by her waist.

The rouge was superb on that wild, tawny face!

- And the lamp resigning itself to dying,

as only the fire in the hearth lit the chamber,

each time it gave out a flame in sighing,

it flooded with blood that skin of amber!

THE SNAKE THAT DANCES

How I love to watch, dear indolence,
　　like a bright shimmer,
of fabric, the skin of your elegant
　　　body glimmer!

Over the bitter-tasting perfume,
　　the depths of your hair,
odorous, restless spume,
　　blue, and brown, waves, there,

like a vessel that stirs, awake
　　when dawn winds rise,
my dreaming soul sets sail
　　for those distant skies.

Your eyes where nothing's revealed
　　either acrid or sweet,
are two cold jewels where steel
　　and gold both meet.

Seeing your rhythmic advance,

    your fine abandon,

one might speak of a snake that danced

    at the end of the branch it's on.

Under its burden of languidness,

    your head at a child-like slant,

rocks with weak listlessness

    like a young elephant's,

and your body heels and stretches

    like some trim vessel,

that, rocking from side to side, plunges

    its yards in the swell.

As when the groaning glacier's thaw

    fills the flowing stream,

so when your mouth's juices pour

    to the tip of your teeth,

I fancy I'm drinking overpowering, bitter,

    Bohemian wine,

that over my heart will scatter

    its stars, a liquid sky!

'JE T'ADORE A L'EGAL DE LA VOUTE NOCTURNE'

I adore you, the nocturnal vault's likeness,

o vast taciturnity, o vase of sadness:

I love you, my beauty, the more you flee,

grace of my nights, the more you seem,

to multiply distances, ah ironically,

that bar my arms from the blue immensity.

I advance to the attack, climb to the assault

like a swarm of worms attacking a corpse,

and I cherish, o creature cruel, and implacable,

your coldness that makes you, for me, more beautiful!

A ROTTING CARCASE

My soul, do you remember the object we saw
on what was a fine summer's day:
at the path's far corner, a shameful corpse
on the gravel-bed, darkly lay,

legs in the air, like a lecherous woman,
burning and oozing with poisons,
revealing, with nonchalance, cynicism,
the belly ripe with its exhalations.

The sun shone down on that rot and mould,
as if to grill it completely,
and render to Nature a hundredfold
what she'd once joined so sweetly:

and the sky gazed at that noble carcass,
like a flower, now blossoming.
The stench was so great, that there, on the grass,
you almost considered fainting.

The flies buzzed away on its putrid belly,

    from which black battalions slid,

larvae, that flowed in thickening liquid

    the length of those seething shreds.

All of the thing rose and fell like a wave,

    surging and glittering:

you'd have said the corpse, swollen with vague

    breath, multiplied, was living.

And that 'world' gave off a strange music,

    like the wind, or the flowing river,

or the grain, tossed and turned with a rhythmic

    motion, by the winnower.

Its shape was vanishing, no more than a dream,

    a slowly-formed rough sketch

on forgotten canvas, the artist's gleam

    of memory alone perfects.

From behind the rocks a restless bitch

    glared with an angry eye,

judging the right moment to snatch

    some morsel she'd passed by.

- And yet you too will resemble that ordure,

    that terrible corruption,

star of my eyes, sun of my nature,

    my angel, and my passion!

Yes! Such you'll become, o queen of grace,

    after the final sacraments,

when you go under the flowering grass

    to rot among the skeletons.

O my beauty! Tell the worms, then, as

    with kisses they eat you away,

how I preserved the form, divine essence

    of my loves in their decay !

BEATRICE

Through fields of ash, burnt, without verdure,

where I was complaining one day to Nature,

and slowly sharpened the knife of my thought,

as I wandered aimlessly, against my heart,

I saw descend, at noon, on my brow,

a storm-filled and sinister cloud,

holding a vicious demonic horde,

resembling cruel, and curious dwarfs.

Gazing at me, considering me, as cool

as passers-by admiring a fool,

I heard them laughing and whispering in synch,

exchanging many a nudge and a wink:

' Let's contemplate this caricature,

this Hamlet's shadow, echoing his posture,

his indecisive looks, and wild hair.

It's a shame to see that epicure there,

that pauper, that actor on holiday, that droll

fellow, because he can play a fine role,

trying to interest with his tears

the eagles, the grasshoppers, streams and flowers,

and even proclaiming his public tirades

to us who invented those ancient parades?'

I might (since my pride, high as the mountains,

overtops clouds and the cries of demons)

simply have turned my regal head,

if I'd not seen, to that obscene crowd wed,

a crime that failed to make the sun rock,

the queen of my heart, with her matchless look,

laughing with them at my dark distress,

and now and then yielding a filthy caress.

THE BALCONY

Mother of memories, mistress of mistresses,
O you, all my pleasures! O you, all my learning!
You will remember the joy of caresses,
the sweetness of home and the beauty of evening,
Mother of memories, mistress of mistresses!

On evenings lit by the glow of the ashes
and on the balcony, veiled, rose-coloured, misted,
how gentle your breast was, how good your heart to me!
We have said things meant for eternity,
on evenings lit by the glow of the ashes.

How lovely the light is on sultry evenings!
How deep the void grows! How powerful the heart is!
As I leaned towards you, queen of adored ones
I thought I breathed perfume from your blood's kiss.
How lovely the light is on sultry evenings!

The night it was thickening and closing around us,

and my eyes in the dark were divining your glance,

and I drank your nectar. Oh sweetness! Oh poison!

your feet held, here, in these fraternal hands.

The night it was thickening and closing around us.

I know how to summon up happiest moments,

and relive my past, there, curled, touching your knees.

What good to search for your languorous beauties

but in your dear body, and your heart so sweet?

I know how to summon up happiest moments!

Those vows, those perfumes, those infinite kisses,

will they be reborn, from gulfs beyond soundings,

as the suns that are young again climb in the sky,

after they've passed through the deepest of drownings?

– O vows! O perfumes! O infinite kisses!

EXOTIC PERFUME

When, in Autumn, on a sultry evening,
eyes closed, I breathe your warm breasts' odour,
I see the shore of bliss uncovered,
in the monotonous sun's fierce gleaming:

a languorous island where Nature has come,
bringing rare trees and luscious fruits:
the bodies of lean and vigorous brutes,
and women with eyes of astounding freedom.

Led by your odour to magic climes
I see a harbour, of masts, sails, lines,
worn down by the sea's waves still,

while the green tamarinds' perfume mounts,
circling in air, and filling my nostrils,
and blends, in my soul, with the sailors' chants.

THE HEAD OF HAIR

O fleece, billowing down to the shoulders!
O curls! O perfume charged with languor!
Ecstasy! To populate love's dark alcove,
with memories sleeping tonight in your hair,
I'd wave it, like a handkerchief, in the air!

Languid Asia and burning Africa,
absent worlds, far-off, almost dead,
live in your forest-depths of aromas!
As music floats other spirits away,
mine, my love, sails your fragrance instead.

I'll go where, full of sap, trees and men
Swoon endlessly in that ardent climate:
Thick tresses, be my tide! You contain,
O sea of ebony, the dazzling dream,
of masts, flames, sails, and oarsmen:

an echoing port where my soul's a drinker

of sound, colour, scent in rolling waves:

where vessels, gliding through silk and amber,

open wide their arms to clasp the splendour

of a pure sky quivering with eternal day.

I'll plunge my head, in love with drunkenness,

in this dark ocean which encloses the other:

and my subtle spirit the breakers caress

will know how to find you, fertile indolence!

Infinite lullaby, full of the balm of leisure!

Hair of blue, that hangs like a shadowy tent,

you bring me the round, immense sky's azure:

in your plaited tresses' feathery descent

I grow fervently drunk with the mingled scent

of coconut-oil, of musk, and coal-tar.

Now! Always! My hand in your heavy mane sowing

jewels, the sapphire, the pearl, and the ruby,

so that you'll not remain deaf to my longing!

Oasis of dream, the gourd where I'm drinking,

of you, long draughts of the wine of memory?

A PHANTOM II: THE PERFUME

R eader, have you ever breathed deeply,
with slow savour and intoxicated sense,
a church's saturating grain of incense,
or the long-lasting musk in a sachet?

Profound magical spell where we
are drunk on the past restored in the present.
So lovers on an adored body scent
the exquisite flower of memory.

From her pliant and heavy hair,
living sachet, censer of the alcoves,
a fragrance, wild and savage, rose,

and from her clothes, velvet or muslin, there,
impregnated with her pure years,
emanated a perfume of furs.

AFTERNOON SONG

Though your eyebrows surprise,

and give you an air of strangeness,

which isn't that of the angels,

witch with seductive eyes,

I adore my frivolous girl,

my terrible passion,

with the devotion

of a priest for his idol!

The forest and the desert

perfume your wild hair:

your head has an air

of the enigma, the secret.

Round your flesh, perfume sweet

swirls like a censer's cloud:

you bewitch like the twilight's shroud,

nymph of shadows and heat.

Ah! The strongest potions made

can't match your idleness,

and you know the caress

that resurrects the dead.

Your hips are enamoured

of your back and your breasts,

and the cushions are ravished

with your poses, so languid.

Sometimes to appease

your rage, mysteriously,

you lavish, gravely

your bites and your kisses.

You tear me, my dark-haired one,

with a mocking smile's art,

and then cast on my heart

your gaze sweet as the moon.

Under your shoes so satiny,

your graceful silken feet,

I lay my genius, my wit,

my joy, and my destiny,

restorer of my health's sweetness,

you, all colour and light,

explosion of warmth, bright

in my Siberian darkness.

THE DEATH OF LOVERS

We will have beds filled with light scent, and
couches deep as a tomb,
and strange flowers in the room,
blooming for us under skies so pleasant.

Vying to exhaust their last fires
our hearts will be two vast flares,
reflecting their double glares
in our two spirits, twin mirrors.

One evening of mystic blue and rose
we'll exchange a single brief glow
like a long sob, heavy with goodbye,

and later, opening the doors, the angel who came
faithful and joyful, will revive
the lustreless mirrors, and the lifeless flame.

THE FLAWED BELL

It's bitter, yet sweet, on wintry nights,
near to the fire that crackles and fumes,
listening while, far-off, slow memories rise
to echoing chimes that ring through the gloom.

Lucky indeed, the loud-tongued bell
still hale and hearty despite its age,
repeating its pious call, true and well,
like an old trooper in the sentry's cage!

My soul is flawed: when, at boredom's sigh,
it would fill the chill night air with its cry,
it often happens that its voice, enfeebled,

thickens like a wounded man's death-rattle
by a lake of blood, vast heaps of the dying,
who ends, without moving, despite his trying.

THE OWLS

Among the black yews, their shelter,
the owls are ranged in a row,
like alien deities, the glow,
of their red eyes pierces. They ponder.

They perch there without moving,
till that melancholy moment
when quenching the falling sun,
the shadows are growing.

Their stance teaches the wise
to fear, in this world of ours,
all tumult, and all movement:

Mankind, drunk on brief shadows,
always incurs a punishment
for his longing to stir, and go.

TO A RED-HEADED BEGGAR-GIRL

Pale girl with fiery hair,

whose tattered dress shows there

glimpses of your poverty

and your beauty,

a wretched poet, for me,

your young skinny body

with its freckled brownness

has its sweetness.

You wear, more stylishly

than a queen in story

wears her velvet shoe

your heavy two.

Instead of your dress, ripped, short,

may a fine robe of court

trail in long folds to greet

your slender feet:

in place of your torn hose

may daggers of gold,

down your legs, blaze

    for the eyes of roués:

may ribbons loosely tied

unveil in your pride

your two lovely breasts, bright

    as your eyes:

may your arms be coaxed too,

to sweetly undress you,

and with pert blows

    discourage those

impish fingers, pearls that glow,

sonnets of master Belleau,

by your captive lovers,

    endlessly offered.

The poets, in pursuit,

dedicating to you their fruit,

and gazing at your shoes, there

    from beneath the stair:

many a page-boy's game,

many a famous name,

would spy, still hoping,

    on your cool lodging!

You, in your bed, would count

more kisses than lilies no doubt,

and subject to your law

    a Valois or more!

- Meanwhile you go seeking

any old scraps, cadging,

outside the back door

    of some shabby store:

you go gazing, from afar,

at valueless beads that are

still, alas, so much more

    than I can afford!

Go then, with no ornament,

perfume, pearl or diamond,

only your slender nudity,

    O my beauty!

WANDERING GYPSIES

The prophetic tribe with burning eyes
yesterday took to the highway, carrying
children slung on their backs, or offering
proud hunger the breast's ever-ripe prize.

The men go on foot, with shining weapons,
by the carts where their folk huddle together,
sweeping the heavens, eyes grown heavier
with mournful regret for absent visions.

The cricket, deep in his sandy retreat,
redoubles his call, on seeing their passing feet:
Cybele, who loves them, re-leafs the glades,

makes the rocks gush, the desert bloom,
before these voyagers, thrown wide to whom
is the intimate kingdom of future shades.

Note: Cybele was the Phrygian great goddess, personifying the earth in its savage state, worshipped in caves and on mountaintops.

BAD LUCK

To roll the rock you fought

takes your courage, Sisyphus!

No matter what effort from us,

Art is long, and Time is short.

Far from the grave of celebrity,

my heart, like a muffled drum,

taps out its funereal thrum

towards some lonely cemetery.

— Many a long-buried gem

sleeps in shadowy oblivion

far from pickaxes and drills:

in profound solitude set,

many a flower, with regret,

its sweet perfume spills.

THE DEATH OF THE POOR

It is Death, alas, persuades us to keep on living:
the goal of life and the only hope we have,
like an elixir, rousing, intoxicating, giving
the strength to march on towards the grave:

through the frost and snow and storm-wind, look
it's the vibrant light on our black horizon:
the fabulous inn, written of in the book,
where one can eat, and sleep and sit oneself down:

it's an Angel, who holds in his magnetic beams,
sleep and the gift of ecstatic dreams,
who makes the bed where the poor and naked lie:

it's the glory of the Gods, the mystic granary,
it's the poor man's purse, his ancient country,
it's the doorway opening on an unknown sky!

MUSIC

Music, like an ocean, often carries me away!
    Through the ether far,
or under a canopy of mist, I set sail
    for my pale star.

Breasting the waves, my lungs swollen
    like a ship's canvas,
night veils from me the long rollers,
    I ride their backs:

I sense all a suffering vessel's passions
    vibrating within me:
while fair winds or the storm's convulsions

    on the immense deep
cradle me. Or else flat calm, vast mirror there
    of my despair!

THE RANSOM

Man, with which to pay his ransom,
has two fields of deep rich earth,
which he must dig and bring to birth,
with the iron blade of reason.

To obtain the smallest rose,
to garner a few ears of wheat,
he must wet them without cease,
with briny tears from his grey brow.

One is Art: Love is the other.
- To render his propitiation,
on the day of conflagration,
when the last strict reckoning's here,

full of crops' and flowers' displays
he will have to show his barns,
with those colours and those forms
that gain the Angels' praise.

VOYAGE TO CYTHERA

My heart soared with joy, like a bird in flight,
haunting the rigging sliding by:
the ship swayed under a cloudless sky,
like an angel, dazed by radiant light.

What island is that, dark and sad? - Cythera,
in verse, it's famous you understand,
every aged child's golden land.
Look, after all, there's nothing here.

- Isle of sweet secrets and the heart's delight!
Ancient Venus's marvellous shadow,
like perfume, covers the sea, around you,
fills the mind with love, and the languorous night.

Isle of green myrtle and flowers, wide open,
beautiful, revered by every nation,
where the sighs, of the heart's adoration,
glide like incense, over a rose garden,

or are cooing, like doves, in scented air!

- Cythera, now a desert, to mock,

full of piercing calls, a barren rock.

But I saw a strange thing there!

It was not a temple, shaded by trees,

where the young priestess, with flower-like desires,

her body alight with secret fires,

goes, opening her robes to the passing breeze.

But a shore where our white sails moving by

disturbed the birds, and we saw, like jet,

the black of a cypress tree's silhouette,

a three-branched gibbet, against the sky.

A fierce bird, perching, on the head

of a hanged man, rent him, surely,

planting its impure beak, in fury,

in the bloody corners of the dead.

The eyes were two holes: from the cavernous belly

the weight of his guts poured down his sides,

and his torturers, gorged on hideous delights,

had castrated him, most efficiently.

Beneath his feet, circling, spun a jealous pack

their muzzles lifted, of whirling beasts,

one large one, leaping in their midst,

an executioner, with cohorts at his back.

Inhabitant of Cythera, son, of that lovely sky,

you suffered their insults, silently,

to expiate your infamy,

lacking the tomb your crimes deny.

Hanged man, grotesque sufferer, your pain is mine!

I felt at the sight of your dangling limbs,

the long stream of gall, old sufferings,

rise to my teeth like acid bile.

Before you, poor devil, of dear memory,

I felt all the beaks, and ravening claws,

of swooping ravens, dark panthers' jaws,

that were once so fond of tearing at me.

- The sky was entrancing, so calm the sea,

but, to me, all was dark, and smeared with blood.

Alas! My heart was buried, for good,

in the depths, the winding sheet, of an allegory.

O Venus, what I found, in your island, was just

a symbolic gallows, with my image, in suspense.

O God! Give me the courage, and the strength,

to contemplate my heart, and body, without disgust!

Note: The island of Cythera in the Aegean Sea is the symbolic isle of Venus Aphrodite, who was born from the sea-foam, near the island.

EVENING TWILIGHT

Here's the criminal's friend, delightful evening:
come like an accomplice, with a wolf's loping:
slowly the sky's vast vault hides each feature,
and restless man becomes a savage creature.

Evening, sweet evening, desired by him who can say
without his arms proving him a liar: 'Today
we've worked!' – It refreshes, this evening hour,
those spirits that savage miseries devour,
the dedicated scholar with heavy head,
the bowed workman stumbling home to bed.
Yet now unhealthy demons rise again
clumsily, in the air, like busy men,
beat against sheds and arches in their flight.
And among the wind-tormented gas-lights
Prostitution switches on through the streets
opening her passageways like an ant-heap:
weaving her secret tunnels everywhere,
like an enemy planning a coup, she's there
burrowing into the wombs of the city's mires,
like a worm stealing from Man what it desires.

Here, there, you catch the kitchens' whistles,

the orchestras' droning, the theatres' yells,

low dives where gambling's all the pleasure,

filling with whores, and crooks, their partners,

and the thieves who show no respite or mercy,

will soon be setting to work, as they tenderly,

they too, toil at forcing safes and doorways,

to live, clothe their girls, for a few more days.

Collect yourself, my soul, at this grave hour,

and close your ears to the rising howl.

It's now that the pains of the sick increase!

Dark Night clasps them by the throat: they reach

their journey's end, the common pit's abandon:

the hospital fills with their sighs. – Many a one,

will never return to their warm soup by the fire,

by the hearth, at evening, next to their heart's desire.

And besides the majority have never known

never having lived, the gentleness of home!

MORNING TWILIGHT

Reveille was sounding on barrack-squares,
and the wind of dawn blew on lighted stairs.

It was the hour when a swarm of evil visions

torments swarthy adolescents, when pillows hum:

when, a bloodshot eye, throbbing and quivering,

the lamp makes a reddened stain on the morning:

when the soul, by dull sour body, bowed down,

enacts the struggle between lamp and dawn.

Like a tearful face that the breeze wipes dry,

the air's filled with the *frisson* of things that fly,

and man is tired of writing, woman with loving.

The chimneys, here and there, began smoking.

The women of pleasure, with their bleary eyes,

and gaping mouths, were sleeping stupefied:

poor old women, with chilled and meagre breasts,

blew the embers, then fingers, roused from rest.

It was the hour, when frozen, with money scarcer,

the pains of women in childbirth grew fiercer:

and like a sob cut short by a surge of blood

a cock-crow far away broke through the fog:

a sea of mist bathed the buildings, dying men,

in the depths of the workhouse, groaned again

emitting their death-rattles in ragged breaths.

Debauchees, tired by their efforts, headed for rest.

Shivering dawn in a robe of pink and green

made her way slowly along the deserted Seine,

and sombre Paris, eyes rubbed and watering,

groped for its tools, an old man, labouring.

THE INVITATION TO THE VOYAGE

My sister, my child
imagine, exiled,

The sweetness, of being there, we two!

To live and to sigh,

to love and to die,

In the land that mirrors you!

The misted haze

of its clouded days

Has the same charm to my mind,

as mysterious,

as your traitorous

Eyes, behind glittering blinds.

There everything's order and beauty,

calm, voluptuousness, and luxury.

The surface gleams

are polished it seems,

Through the years, to grace our room.

The rarest flowers

mix, with fragrant showers,

The vague, amber perfume.

The dark, painted halls,

the deep mirrored walls,

With Eastern splendour hung,

all secretly speak,

to the soul, its discrete,

Sweet, native tongue.

There, everything's order and beauty,

calm, voluptuousness and luxury.

See, down the canals,

the sleeping vessels,

Those nomads, their white sails furled:

Now, to accomplish

your every wish,

They come from the ends of the world.

- The deep sunsets

surround the west,

The canals, the city, entire,

with blue-violet and gold;

and the Earth grows cold

In an incandescent fire.

There, everything's order and beauty,

calm, voluptuousness and luxury.

THE INVITATION TO THE VOYAGE (PROSE POEM)

There's a magnificent land, a land of Cockaigne, they say, that I've dreamed of visiting with a dear mistress. A unique land, drowned in our Northern mists, that you might call the Orient of the West, the China of Europe, so freely is warm and capricious Fantasy expressed there, so patiently and thoroughly has she adorned it with learned and luxuriant plants.

A true land of Cockaigne, where all is lovely, rich, tranquil, honest: where luxury delights in reflecting itself as order: where life is full and sweet to breathe: from which disorder, turbulence, the unforeseen are banished: where happiness is married to silence: where the cooking itself is poetic, both rich and exciting: where everything resembles you, my sweet angel.

Do you know that fevered malady that seizes us in our cold misery, that nostalgia for an unknown land, that anguish of curiosity? There's a country you resemble, where everything is lovely, tranquil and honest, where Fantasy has built and adorned a western China, where life is sweet to breathe, where happiness is married to silence. There we must go and live, there we must go to die!

Yes, there we must go to breathe, dream, prolong the hours with an infinity of sensations. Some musician has composed *The Invitation to the Waltz*: who shall compose *The Invitation to the Voyage*, one can offer to the beloved, the sister of their choice?

Yes, it would be good to be alive in that atmosphere, - there where the hours that pass more slowly contain more thought, where the clocks chime happiness with a deeper, more significant solemnity.

On shining wall-panels, on walls lined with gilded leather, of sombre richness, blissful paintings live discreetly, calm and deep as the souls of the artists who created them. The sunsets that colour the dining-room, the salon, so richly, are softened by fine fabrics, or those high latticed windows divided in sections by leading. The furniture, vast, curious, bizarre, is armed with locks and secrets like refined souls. The mirrors, metals, fabrics, plate and ceramics play a mute, mysterious symphony for the eyes: and from every object, every corner, the gaps in the drawers, the folds of fabric, a unique perfume escapes: the call of Sumatra, that is like the soul of the apartment.

A true land of Cockaigne, I tell you, where all is rich, clean and bright like a clear conscience, like a splendid battery of kitchenware, like magnificent jewellery, like a multi-coloured gem! The treasures of the world enrich it, as in the home of some hard-working man, who's deserved well of the whole world. A unique land, superior to others, as art is to Nature, re-shaped here by dream, corrected, adorned, remade.

Let them search and search again, tirelessly extending the frontiers of their happiness, those alchemists of the gardener's art! Let them offer sixty, a hundred thousand florins reward to whoever realises their ambitious projects! I though, have found my *black tulip*, my *blue dahlia*!

Incomparable bloom, tulip re-found, allegorical dahlia, it is there, is it not, to that beautiful land so calm and full of dreams, that you must go to live and flower? Would you not be surrounded by your own analogue, could you not mirror yourself, to speak as the mystics do, in your own *correspondence*?

Dreams! Always dreams! And the more aspiring and fastidious the soul, the more its dreams exceed the possible. Every man has within him his does of natural opium, endlessly secreted and renewed, and how many hours do we count, from birth to death, that are filled with positive pleasure, by successful deliberate action? Shall we ever truly live, ever enter this picture my mind has painted, this picture that resembles you?

Those treasures, items of furniture, that luxury, order, those perfumes, miraculous flowers, are you. They are you also, those great rivers and tranquil canals. Those huge ships they carry charged with riches, from which rise monotonous sailors chants, those are my thoughts that sleep or glide over your breast. You conduct them gently towards that sea, the Infinite, while reflecting the depths of the sky in your sweet soul's clarity: - and when, wearied by the swell, gorged with Oriental wares, they re-enter their home port, they are my thoughts still, enriched, returning from the Infinite to you.

THE IRREPARABLE

Can we stifle the old, long-lived Remorse,
that lives, writhes, heaves,
feeds on us, like a worm on a corpse,
like oak-gall on the oak-trees?
Can we stifle the old, long-lived Remorse?

In what potion, in what wine, in what brew,
shall we drown this old enemy.
greedy, destructive as a prostitute,
ant-like always filled with tenacity?
In what potion? – In what wine? – In what brew?

Tell us, lovely witch, oh, tell us, if you know,
tell the spirit filled with anguish
as if dying crushed by the wounded, oh,
crumpled beneath the horses,
tell us, lovely witch, oh, tell us, if you know,

tell the one in agony the wolf's already scented

    whom the raven now surveys,

tell the shattered soldier! Say, if he's intended

    to despair of cross and grave:

poor soul in agony the wolf's already scented!

Can we illuminate a black and muddied sky?

    can we pierce the shadowy evening,

denser than pitch, with neither day or night,

    star-less, with no funereal lightning?

Can we illuminate a black and muddied sky?

The Hope that shone in the Tavern window

    is quenched, is dead forever!

How to find without sunlight, without moon-glow,

    for the foul road's martyrs, ah, shelter!

The Devil's quenched all in the Tavern window!

Adorable witch, do you love the damned?

    Say, do you know the unforgivable?

Do you understand Remorse, its poisoned hand,

    for which our heart serves as target?

Adorable witch, do you love the damned?

The Irreparable, with its accursed tooth bites

    at our soul, this pitiful monument,

and often gnaws away like a termite,

    below the foundations of the battlement.

The Irreparable, with its accursed tooth, bites!

- Sometimes on the boards of a cheap stage

    lit up by the sonorous orchestra,

I've seen a fairy kindling miraculous day,

    in the infernal sky above her:

sometimes on the boards of a cheap stage,

a being, who is nothing but light, gold, gauze,

    flooring the enormous Satan:

but my heart, that no ecstasy ever saw,

    is a stage where ever and again

one awaits in vain the Being with wings of gauze!

THE POISON

Wine can clothe the most sordid hole
    in miraculous luxury,
and let many a fabulous portico float free
    in the gold of its red glow,
like a setting sun in the sky's cloudy sea.

Opium expands things without boundaries,
    extends the limitless,
makes time profounder, deepens voluptuousness,
    fills the soul beyond its capacities,
with the pleasures of gloom and of darkness.

None of that equals the poison that flows
    from your eyes, your eyes of green,
lakes where, mirrored, my trembling soul is seen...
    my dreams come flocking, a host,
to quench their thirst in the bitter stream.

None of that equals the dreadful marvel though

    of your saliva's venom,

that plunges my soul, remorseless, into oblivion,

    and causing vertigo,

rolls it swooning towards the shores of doom!

CLOUDED SKY

One would say your gaze was a misted screen:
your strange eyes (are they blue, grey or green?)
changeable, tender, dreamy, cruel, and again
echoing the indolence and pallor of heaven.

You bring me those blank days, mild and hazy,
that melt bewitched hearts into weeping,
when twisted, stirred by some unknown hurt,
our over-stretched nerves mock the numbed spirit.

Often you resemble the loveliest horizons
lit by the suns of foggy seasons....
how splendid you are, a dew-wet country,
inflamed by the rays of a misted sky!

O dangerous woman, o seductive glow,
will I someday adore your frost and snow,
and learn to draw, from implacable winter
sharp-edged as steel or ice, new pleasure?

THE CAT

I

A fine cat prowls about in my brain,
as if in his own apartment,
he's charming, gentle, confident,
when he mews you have to strain

to hear the discreet and tender tone:
whether it soothes or scolds its sound
is always rich, always profound.
It's his secret charm, and his alone.

This voice which purls and filters
to the darkest depths of my being
swells in me like verse multiplying
and delights me like a magic philtre.

It comprehends all ecstasy,
calms my cruellest suffering:
and has no need of words to sing
the longest sentences to me.

No, there's no bow that gliding

over my heart's pure instrument,

could make its most sensitive string

deliver more noble tidings,

than your voice, which as

in an angel, cat of mystery,

seraphic, extraordinary,

is as subtle as it's harmonious!

II

From its light-brownish fur, such

a sweet perfume gathers,

I was scented by it after

stroking it once, one touch.

It's the room's familiar spirit:

it judges, presides, inspires,

all things within its empire:

a god perhaps, a faery is it?

When my eyes are obediently

drawn to this cat I love,

like a magnet, and I look

into myself profoundly,

I see with pure amazement

the fire of his pale pupils,

bright lamps, living opals,

fixed on me, in contemplation.

MONOLOGUE

You are a lovely autumn sky, rose-clear!
But sadness is flowing in me like the sea,
And leaves on my sullen lip, as it disappears,
of its bitter slime the painful memory.

– Your hand glides over my numb breast in vain:
what it seeks, dear friend, is a place made raw
by woman's ferocious fang and claw, refrain:
seek this heart, the wild beasts tear, no more.

My heart is a palace defiled by the rabble,
they drink, and murder, and clutch each other's hair!
– About your naked throat a perfume hovers!...

O Beauty, harsh scourge of souls, this is your care!
With your eyes of fire, dazzling as at our feasts,
Burn these scraps to ashes, spared by the beasts!

AUTUMN SONG

I

Soon we'll plunge into the bitter shadows:
Goodbye bright sunlit summers, all too short!
Already I can hear the gloomy blows:
the wood reverberates in some paved court.

Winter once more will enter in my being: anger,
shuddering, horror, hate, forced labour's shock,
like the sun in its deep hell, northern, polar,
my heart no more than a red, frozen block.

Trembling, I hear every log that falls:
building a scaffold makes no duller echoes.
My spirit's like a shattered tower, its walls
split by the battering ram's slow tireless blows.

Rocked by monotonous thuds, I feel it's done,
a coffin's being nailed in haste somewhere.
For whom? – Yesterday summer, now it's autumn!
The mysterious noise rings of departure there.

II

I love the greenish light of your almond eyes,

gentle beauty, but all's bitter to me today,

and nothing, your love, the boudoir, your fire,

matches the sun, for me, glittering on the waves.

Yet tender heart, love me still! Be like a mother

however ungrateful, however unworthy I am:

be the short-lived sweetness, sister or lover,

of a glorious autumn or the setting sun.

Short task! The grave waits: it is greedy!

Ah, let me rest my forehead on your knees,

regretting summer, white and torrid, let me

enjoy the late season's gentle yellow rays!

AUTUMN SONNET

Your eyes, clear as crystal, ask me: 'Strange lover,
what do I mean to you?'- Hush, and be charming!
My heart, irritated by all but the one thing,
the primitive creature's absolute candour,

is unwilling to show its infernal secret to you,
cradler whose hand invites to deep slumber,
and its black inscription written in fire,
I hate passion, the spirit sickens me too!

Let us love gently. Love in hiding, discreet,
in shadowy ambush, bends his fatal bow.
The weapons of his ancient arsenal I know:

Crime, horror, madness! – My pale marguerite!
are you not, as I am, an autumn sun though,
O my so white, my so cold Marguerite?

TO SHE WHO IS TOO LIGHT-HEARTED

Your head, your gesture, your air,
are lovely, like a lovely landscape:
laughter's alive, in your face,
a fresh breeze in a clear atmosphere.

The dour passer-by you brush past there,
is dazzled by health in flight,
flashing like a brilliant light
from your arms and shoulders.

The resounding colours
with which you sprinkle your dress,
inspire the spirits of poets
with thoughts of dancing flowers.

Those wild clothes are the emblem
of your brightly-hued mind:
madcap by whom I'm terrified,
I hate you, and love you, the same!

Sometimes in a lovely garden

where I trailed my listlessness,

I've felt the sunlight sear my breast

like some ironic weapon:

and Spring's green presence

brought such humiliation

I've levied retribution on

a flower, for Nature's insolence.

So through some night, when the hour

of sensual pleasure sounds,

I'd like to slink, mute coward, bound

for your body's treasure,

to bruise your sorry breast,

to punish your joyful flesh,

form in your startled side, a fresh

wound's yawning depth,

and — breath-taking rapture! —

through those lips, new and full

more vivid and more beautiful

infuse my venom, my sister!

REVERSIBILITY

Angel of joyfulness, do you know anguish,

shame, remorse, sobbing, despondency,

those dreadful nights of vague anxiety,

when, like crumpled paper, the heart's crushed?

Angel of joyfulness, do you know anguish,

Angel of goodness, do you know hatred,

fists clenched in the darkness, tears of gall,

when vengeance taps out its infernal call,

and takes control of thoughts in the head?

Angel of goodness, do you know hatred?

Angel of health, do you know the fevers,

that the length of the dingy workhouse wall,

like exiles, dragging their feet along, all

moving their lips, seek absent summers?

Angel of health, do you know the fevers?

Angel of beauty, do you know those furrows,

and fears of old-age, and the hideous torture

of reading devotion's intimate horror,

in eyes where for years our greedy eyes burrowed?

Angel of beauty, do you know those furrows?

Angel of happiness, of joy's bright flares,

King David would have found life, near the tomb,

in your enchanted body's perfume:

but, angel, all I ask of you is your prayers,

Angel of happiness, of joy's bright flares!

Note: The servants of King David sought for a young virgin to warm him in his old age, because he could get no heat. See The First Book of Kings 1-4.

CONFESSION

Once, once only, sweet and lovable woman,
    you leant your smooth arm on mine
(that memory has never faded a moment
    from the shadowy depths of my mind):

it was late: the full moon spread its light
    like a freshly minted disc,
and like a river, the solemnity of night
    flowed over sleeping Paris.

Along the houses, under carriage gates,
    cats crept past furtively,
ears pricked, or else like familiar shades,
    accompanied us slowly.

Suddenly, in our easy intimacy,
    that flower of the pale light,
from you, rich, sonorous instrument, eternally
    quivering gaily, bright,

from you, clear and joyous as a fanfare

    in the glittering dawn

a strange, plaintive sigh escaped

    a faltering tone

as from some stunted child, detestable, sullen, foul,

    whose family in shame

hide it for years, to conceal it from the world

    in the cellar's dark cave.

My poor angel, that harsh voice of yours cried:

    'That nothing on earth is certain,

and however carefully it's disguised,

    human selfishness rips the curtain:

it's a hard life being a lovely woman,

    it's the banal occupation

of a cold, crazed dancer who summons

    the mechanical smile's occasion:

it's stupid to build on the mortal heart:

    everything shatters, love and beauty,

till Oblivion hurls them into its cart,

    and returns them to Eternity!'

I've often recalled that enchanted silence,

its moon, and its languor: all

of that dreadful whispered confidence

in the heart's confessional.

FOR MADAME SABATIER

What will you say tonight, poor soul in solitude,
what will you say my heart, withered till now,
to the so beautiful, so sweet, so dear one,
whose divine gaze recreated the flower?

- We will set Pride now to singing her praises:
nothing outdoes her sweet air of authority.
Her spiritual flesh has the perfume of angels,
and her eye surrounds us in robes of infinity.

Whether in the night, and alone, and in solitude,
whether in the street, and among the multitude,
her phantom dances in air, like a flame.

Sometimes it speaks and it says 'I am beautiful.
You, for the love of me, must love beauty alone:
for I am your Madonna, Muse, Guardian Angel.

THE LIVING TORCH

They go before me, those Eyes full of light
that some wise Angel has magnetised,
those divine brothers, my brothers, go, bright,
flashing their diamond fires in my eyes.

Leading my steps on Beauty's way,
saving me from snares, from grievous crime,
they are my servants and I am their slave:
all my being obeys that living flame.

Charmed Eyes, you shine with the mystic glow
of candles lighted in broad day, the sun
reddens, fails to quench, their eerie flow:

they celebrate Death: you sing the Resurrection:
you sing the resurrection of my soul,
Stars whose fires no sun can ever cool!

HYMN

To the too-dear, to the too-beautiful,
who fills my heart with clarity,
to the angel, to the immortal idol,
All hail, in immortality!

She flows through my reality,
air, mixed with the salt sea-swell:
into my soul's ecstasy,
pours the essence of the eternal;

Ever-fresh sachet, that scents
the dear corner's atmospheric light,
hidden smoke, of the burning censer,
in the secret paths of night.

How, incorruptible love,
to express your endless verities?
Grain of musk, unseen, above,
in the depths of my infinities!

To the too-dear, to the too-beautiful,

who is my joy and sanity,

to the angel, to the immortal idol,

All hail in immortality!

MOESTA ET ERRABUNDA

Tell me, does your heart sometimes soar, Agathe,
far from the dark sea of the sordid city,
towards another sea, a blaze of splendour that
is blue, bright, deep as virginity?
Tell me, does your heart sometimes soar, Agathe?

The sea, the vast sea, consoles us for our efforts!
What demon entrusted the sea, that hoarse singer
that accompanies the immense roar of tempests,
with being the sublime sleep-bringer?
The sea, the vast sea, consoles us for our efforts!

Carry me wagons! Take me, frigate!
Far, far! Here the city slime is made of our weeping!
Is it true that your sad heart, Agathe,
cries: 'Far from remorse, from crime, from suffering,
carry me wagons, take me frigate!

How far perfumed paradise, you are removed

from us, where the clear blue is all love and happiness,

where what one loves is worthy of being loved,

where the heart drowns in pure voluptuousness!

How far, perfumed paradise, you are removed!

But the green paradise of childhood's thrill,

the games, the songs, the kisses, and the flowers,

the violin making music behind the hill,

and the wine glass, under the trees, in twilight hours,

- But the green paradise of childhood's thrill,

the innocent paradise full of secret yearning,

is it already further than India or China?

Can we call it back, with cries of longing,

and re-create it, with its voice of silver,

the innocent paradise full of secret yearning?

Note: Moesta et Errabunda: Sad and Restless. 'Agathe' is pronounced as 'Agat', to rhyme with 'that'.

HARMONY OF EVENING

Now those days arrive when, stem throbbing,
each flower sheds its fragrance like a censer:
sounds and scents twine in the evening air:
languorous dizziness, Melancholy dancing!

Each flower sheds its fragrance like a censer:
the violin quivers, a heart that's suffering:
languorous dizziness, Melancholy dancing!
the sky is lovely, sad like a huge altar.

The violin quivers, a heart that's suffering:
a heart, hating the vast black void, so tender!
the sky is lovely, sad like a huge altar:
the sun is drowned, in its own blood congealing.

A heart, hating the vast black void, so tender:
each trace of the luminous past it's gathering!
The sun is drowned, in its own blood congealing...
A vessel of the host, your memory shines there.

SEMPER EADEM

'Where does it come from,' you ask, 'this strange sadness,
that climbs, like the sea, over black, bare stone?'
– When our heart has once reaped the harvest,
life is an evil. That's known,

as the simplest of miseries, and nothing mysterious,
and seen by everyone, like your ecstasy.
Stop searching, you, beauty, so curious!
And, though your voice is sweet, sit, silently!

Be quiet, fool! Ever-ravished soul!
Lips of childish laughter! Often, more than the whole
of Life, Death grips us, with subtle ties we have made.

Let me, let my heart, then, be drunk on its lies,
plunge as into a beautiful dream, into your eyes,
and, forever, sleep, in your eyelids' shade.

TO THE READER

Stupidity and error, avarice and vice,

possess our spirits, batten on our flesh,

we feed that fond remorse, our guest,

like ragged beggars nourishing their lice.

Our sins are mulish, our repentance vain:

we make certain our confessions pay,

we'll happily retrace the muddied way,

thinking vile tears will wash away the stain.

Satan Trismegistes rocks the bewitched

Mind, endlessly, on evil's pillow, till,

all the precious metal of our will's

vaporised by that knowing alchemist.

The Devil pulls the strings that make us move!

We take delight in such disgusting things:

one step nearer Hell each new day brings

us, void of horror, to the stinking gloom.

We clutch at furtive pleasure as we pass,

like the debauchee whose lips are pressed

to some antique whore's battered breast,

squeezing the rotten orange that we grasp.

Packed, and seething like a million worms,

a host of Demons riot in our brains,

and when we breathe, invisibly, Death drains

into our lungs, stream full of silent groans.

If poison, arson, knives, base desire,

haven't yet embroidered deft designs

on the dull canvas of our pitiful lives

it's only, alas, because our souls lack fire.

Among the jackals, bitches, panthers,

monkeys, scorpions, serpents, vultures,

that screech, howl, grunt, and crawl, ogres,

in the vile menagerie of our errors,

there's one of uglier, nastier, fouler birth!

Without one wild gesture, one savage yell,

it would willingly send this world to hell,

and in one great yawn swallow up the earth:

it's Boredom! – in its eye's an involuntary tear,

dreaming of scaffolds, as it smokes its *hookah*,

you know it, Reader, that fastidious monster,

hypocrite, Reader, – my brother, – and my peer!

Note: Trismegistes. Baudelaire here fuses the persons of Satan and Hermes Trismegistes (or Trismegistus). The works of Hermes Trismegistes (The Thrice Great), known as the *Corpus Hermeticum* were believed during the Renaissance to be Egyptian but were later attributed to Hellenistic writers of the second century A.D, writing in the style of Plotinus. The *Corpus Hermeticum* takes the form of dialogues between Trismegistus, Thoth, and several other Egyptian deities, including Isis. Little in the text is original. Much of the Hermetic world view is grounded in the philosophy of Plato. Hermetics saw the universe in terms of light and dark, good and evil, spirit and matter. Like their Gnostic contemporaries, practitioners preached mind-body dualism and salvation through the possession of true and divine knowledge.

THE ENEMY

My youth was only a threatening storm,
pierced here and there by glowing heat:
my garden scarcely let a ripe fruit form,
the thunderous rain's destruction is complete.

Now I've reached the autumn of ideas,
I must needs labour with rake and spade,
to reclaim afresh the inundated meres,
where pits were scooped as deep as graves.

Who knows whether the flowers I dream
will find in soil, washed by the salt-stream,
the mystic manna that will give them vigour?

– O Sadness! Sadness! Time eats at our lives,
the unseen Enemy drinks, that gnaws our
heart, our wasted blood, digs in, and thrives!

MIST AND RAIN

Late autumns, winters, spring-times steeped in mud,

anaesthetizing seasons! You I praise, and love

for so enveloping my heart and brain

in vaporous shrouds, in sepulchres of rain.

In this vast landscape where chill south winds play,

where long nights hoarsen the shrill weather-vane,

it opens wide its raven's wings, my soul,

freer than in times of mild renewal.

Nothing's sweeter to my heart, full of sorrows,

on which the hoar-frost fell in some past time,

O pallid seasons, queens of our clime,

than the changeless look of your pale shadows,

- except, two by two, to lay our grief to rest

in some moonless night, on a perilous bed.

LOVER'S WINE

Today Space is fine!
Like a horse mount this wine,
without bridle, spurs, bit,
for a heaven divine!

We, two angels they torture
with merciless fever,
will this mirage pursue
in the day's crystal blue!

Sweetly balanced, fly higher
through the whirlwind's wise air
in our mirrored desire,

my sister, swim there
without rest or respite
to my dream paradise!

THE SOLITARY'S WINE

A flirtatious woman's singular gaze
as she slithers towards you, like the white rays
the vibrant moon throws on the trembling sea

where she wishes to bathe her casual beauty,

the last heap of chips in the gambler's grasp,
skinny Adeline's licentious kiss,
a fragment of music's unnerving caress,
resembling a distant human gasp,

none of these equal, O profound bottle,
the powerful balm of your fecund vessel,
kept for the pious poet's thirsting heart:

you pour out youth, and hope, and life,
and the deepest poverty's treasure – pride,
filling us with triumph, and the Gods' divine art!

THE PIPE

I am the pipe of an author:
from my complexion you can see,
like an Abyssinian girl's ebony,
that my owner's a heavy smoker.

When he's overcome by pain
I'm like the cottage chimney smoking,
where the evening supper's cooking,
for the ploughman home again.

I entwine his soul, and soothe it,
in the blue and swirling veil,
that floats from my mouth, pale

rings of powerful balm around it,
that charm his heart, and bless
his spirit freed from weariness.

THE GAME

Old courtesans in washed-out armchairs,
pale, eyebrows blacked, eyes 'tender', 'fatal',
simpering still, and from their skinny ears
loosing their waterfalls of stone and metal:

Round the green baize, faces without lips,
lips without blood, jaws without the rest,
clawed fingers that the hellish fever grips,
fumbling an empty pocket, heaving breast:

below soiled ceilings, rows of pallid lights,
and huge candelabras shed their glimmer,
across the brooding brows of famous poets:
here it's their blood and sweat they squander:

this the dark tableau of nocturnal dream
my clairvoyant eye once watched unfold.
In an angle of that silent lair, I leaned
hard on my elbows, envious, mute, and cold,

yes, envying that crew's tenacious passion,

the graveyard gaiety of those old whores,

all bravely trafficking to my face, this one

her looks, that one his family honour,

heart scared of envying many a character

fervently rushing at the wide abyss,

drunk on their own blood, who'd still prefer

torment to death, and hell to nothingness!

SPLEEN

I'm like the king of a rain-soaked country,

rich but impotent, young in senility,

who despises his tutors' servile features,

as bored with his dogs as with other creatures.

Nothing enlivens him, hunting or falconry,

or his people dying beside the balcony.

His favourite fool's most grotesque antic

won't calm this brow so cruelly sick:

his fleur-de-lys bed has become a tomb,

his ladies, who give all princes room,

can't invent new dresses so totally wanton

as to raise a smile from this young skeleton.

The alchemist, making him gold, has never

banished from his being the corrupted matter,

or in baths of blood that the Romans gave,

that men of power recall near the grave,

been able to warm that living cadaver,

where instead of blood, runs Lethe's water.

THE VOYAGE

À Maxime du Camp

I

For the child, in love with globe, and stamps,
the universe equals his vast appetite.
Ah! How great the world is in the light of the lamps!
In the eyes of memory, how small and slight!

One morning we set out, minds filled with fire,
travel, following the rhythm of the seas,
hearts swollen with resentment, and bitter desire,
soothing, in the finite waves, our infinities:

Some happy to leave a land of infamies,
some the horrors of childhood, others whose doom,
is to drown in a woman's eyes, their astrologies
the tyrannous Circe's dangerous perfumes.

In order not to become wild beasts, they stun

themselves, with space and light, and skies of fire:

The ice that stings them, and the scorching sun,

slowly erase the marks of their desire.

But the true voyagers are those who leave

only to move: hearts like balloons, as light,

they never swerve from their destinies,

and, without knowing why, say, always: 'Flight!'

Those whose desires take on cloud-likenesses,

who dream of vast sensualities, the same

way a conscript dreams of the guns, shifting vaguenesses,

that the human spirit cannot name.

II

We imitate, oh horror, tops and bowls,

in their leaps and bounds, and even in dreams, dumb

curiosity torments us, and we are rolled,

as if by a cruel Angel that whips the sun!

Strange fate, where the goal never stays the same,

and, belonging nowhere, perhaps it's no matter where

Man, whose hope never tires, as if insane,

rushes on, in search of rest, through the air.

Our soul, a three-master, heads for the isle, of Icarus.

A voice booms, from the bridge 'Skin your eyes!'

A voice, from aloft, eager and maddened, calls to us:

'Love... Fame... Happiness! Hell, it's a rock!' it cries.

On every island, that the lookouts sight,

destiny promises its Eldorado:

Imagination conjuring an orgiastic rite,

finds only a barren reef, in the afterglow.

O, the poor lover of chimeric sands!

Clap him in irons, toss him in the sea,

this drunken sailor, inventing New Found Lands,

whose mirage fills the abyss, with fresh misery?

Like an old tramp, trudging through the mire,

dreaming, head up, of dazzling paradise,

his gaze, bewitched, discovering Capua's fire,

wherever a candlelit hovel meets his eyes.

III

Astounding travellers! What histories

we read in your eyes, deeper than the ocean there!

Show us the treasures of your rich memories,

marvellous jewels made of stars and air.

We wish to voyage without steam or sails!

Project on our spirits, stretched out, like the sheets,

lightening the tedium of our prison tales,

your past, the horizon's furthest reach completes.

Tell us, what did you see?

IV

'We saw the sand,

and waves, we also saw the stars:

despite the shocks, disasters, the unplanned,

we were often just as bored as before.

The sunlight's glory on the violet shoals,

the cities' glory as the sunlight wanes,

kindled that restless longing in our souls,

to plunge into the sky's reflected flames.

The richest cities, the greatest scenes, we found

never contained the magnetic lures,

of those that chance fashioned, in the clouds.

Always desire rent us, on distant shores!

Enjoyment adds strength to our desire.

Desire, old tree, for whom, pleasure is the ground,

while your bark thickens, as you grow higher,

your branches long to touch the sky you sound!

Will you grow forever, mighty tree

more alive than cypress? Though, we have brought, with care,

a few specimens, for your album leaves,

brothers, who find beauty, in objects, from out there!

We have saluted gods of ivory,

thrones, jewelled with constellated gleams,

sculpted palaces, whose walls of faery,

to your bankers, would be ruinous dreams.

Clothes that, to your vision, bring drunkenness,

women with painted teeth and breasts,

juggling savants gliding snakes caress.'

V

And then, what then?

VI

'O, Childishness!
Not to forget the main thing, everywhere,
effortlessly, through this world, we've seen,
from top to bottom of the fatal stair,
the tedious spectacle of eternal sin.

Woman, vile slave, full of pride and foolishness,
adoring herself without laughing, loving without disgust:
Man, greedy tyrant, harsh, lewd, merciless,
slave of that slave, a sewer in the dust.

The torturer who plays; the martyr who sobs;
the feast, perfumed and moist, from the bloody drip;
the poison of power, corrupting the despot;
the crowd, in love with the stupefying whip:

Several religions just like our own,

all climbing heaven. Sanctity,

like an invalid, under the eiderdown,

finding in nails, and hair-shirts, ecstasy:

Drunk with its genius, chattering Humanity,

as mad today as ever, or even worse,

crying to God, in furious agony:

" O, my likeness, my master, take my curse!

And, the least stupid, harsh lovers of Delirium,

fleeing the great herd, guarded by Destiny,

taking refuge in the depths of opium!

- That is the news, from the whole world's country.'

VII

Bitter the knowledge we get from travelling!

Today, tomorrow, yesterday, the world shows what we see,

monotonous and mean, our image beckoning,

an oasis of horror, in a desert of ennui!

Shall we go, or stay? Stay, if you can stay:

Go, if you must. One runs, another crouches, to elude

Time, that vigilant, shadow enemy.

Alas! There are runners for whom nothing is any good,

like Apostles, or wandering Jews,

nothing, no vessel or railway car, they assume,

can flee this vile slave driver; others whose

minds can kill him, without leaving their room.

When, at last he places his foot on our spine, a

hope still stirs, and we can shout: 'Forward!'

Just as when we left for China,

the wind in our hair and our eyes fixed to starboard,

sailing over the Shadowy sea,

with a young traveller's joyous mind.

Do you hear those voices, sadly, seductively,

chanting: 'Over here, if you would find,

the perfumed Lotus! It's here we press

miraculous fruits on which your hopes depend:

Come and be drunk, on the strange sweetness,

of the afternoons, that never end.'

Behind a familiar tongue we see the spectre:

Our Pylades stretches his arms towards our face.

'To renew your heart, swim towards your Electra!'

she calls, whose knees we once embraced.

VIII

O Death, old captain, it is time! Weigh anchor.

This land wearies us, O Death! Take flight!

If the sky and sea are dark as ink's black rancour,

our hearts, as you must know, are filled with light!

Pour out your poison, and dissolve our fears!

Its fire so burns our minds, we yearn, it's true,

to plunge to the Void's depths, Heaven or Hell, who cares?

Into the Unknown's depths, to find the *new*.

Notes: Circe was the sea-nymph of Aeaea, who bewitched the followers of Ulysses, and delayed him on her island (See Homer, Odyssey X). Icarus fell into the Icarian Sea, and gave his name to the Sea and the island of Icaria in the Aegean, after his waxen wings had melted when he flew too near the sun. The wings had been made for the two of them by his father Daedalus, who buried him on the island (See Ovid, Metamorphoses VIII 195). Eldorado was the mythical golden man of Inca Peru, hunted for by the Spaniards, synonymous with an unattainable treasure. Capua was the royal capital of ancient Campania, at the time of the Wars in Latium, described in Virgil's Aeneid. The Lotus was the mythical drug of the Lotus Eaters, whom Ulysses visited (See Homer, Odyssey IX), their land a synonym for the world of languor outside time. Pylades was the friend of Orestes, who helped Orestes in his journey to avenge Agamemnon and return to his sister Electra (See Aeschylus, The Oresteian Trilogy: The Choephori).

THE SEVEN OLD MEN

À Victor Hugo

Ant-like city, city full of dreams,
where the passer-by, at dawn, meets the spectre!
Mysteries everywhere are the sap that streams
through the narrow veins of this great ogre.

One morning, when, on the dreary street,
the buildings all seemed heightened, cold
a swollen river's banks carved out to greet,
(their stage-set mirroring an actor's soul),

the dirty yellow fog that flooded space,
arguing with my already weary soul,
steeling my nerves like a hero, I paced
suburbs shaken by the carts' drum-roll.

Suddenly, an old man in rags, their yellow
mirroring the colour of the rain-filled sky,
whose looks alone prompted alms to flow,
except for the evil glittering of his eye,

appeared. You'd have thought his eyeballs

steeped in gall: his gaze intensified the cold,

and his long beard, as rigid as a sword,

was jutting out like Judas's of old.

He was not bent but broken, his spine

made a sharp right angle with his legs,

so that the stick, perfecting his line,

gave him the awkward shape and step

of three-legged usurer, or sick quadruped.

Wading through snow and mud he went

as if, under his feet, he crushed the dead,

hostile to the world, not just indifferent.

Then his double: beard, eyes, rags, stick, back,

no trait distinguished his centenarian twin:

they marched in step, two ghosts of the Baroque,

sprung from one hell, towards some unknown end.

Was I the butt of some infamous game,

some evil chance, aimed at humiliation?

Since minute by minute, I counted seven,

of that sinister old man's multiplication!

Whoever smiles at my anxiety,

and balks at shivering, the un-fraternal,

consider then, despite their senility,

those seven vile monsters looked eternal!

Could I have lived to see an eighth: yet one

more ironic, fatal, inexorable replication,

loathsome Phoenix, his own father and son?

- I turned my back on that hell-bent procession.

Exasperated, a drunk that sees things doubled,

I stumbled home, slammed the door, terrified,

sick, depressed, mind feverish and troubled,

wounded by mystery, the absurd, outside!

In vain my reason tried to take command,

its efforts useless in the tempest's roar,

my soul, a mastless barge, danced, and danced,

over some monstrous sea without a shore!

THE DIGGING SKELETON

I

In the anatomical plates
displayed on the dusty quays
where many a dry book sleeps
mummified, as in ancient days,

drawings to which the gravity
and skill of some past artist,
despite the gloomy subject
have communicated beauty,

you'll see, and it renders those
gruesome mysteries more complete,
flayed men, and skeletons posed,
farm-hands, digging the soil at their feet.

II

Peasants, dour and resigned,

convicts pressed from the grave,

what's the strange harvest, say,

for which you hack the ground,

bending your backbones there,

flexing each fleshless sinew,

what farmer's barn must you

labour to fill with such care?

Do you seek to show — by that pure,

and terrible, emblem of too hard

a fate! — that even in the bone-yard

the promised sleep's far from sure:

that even the Void's a traitor:

that even Death tells us lies,

that in some land new to our eyes,

we must, perhaps, alas, forever,

and ever, and ever, eternally,

wield there the heavy spade,

scrape the dull earth, its blade

beneath our naked, bleeding feet?

FAR AWAY FROM HERE

This is the sanctuary

where the prettified young lady,

calm, and always ready,

fans her breasts, aglow,

elbow on the pillow,

hears the fountain's flow:

it's the room of Dorothea.

- The breeze and water distantly

sing their song, mingled here

with sobs to soothe the spoiled child's fear.

From tip to toe, most thoroughly,

her delicate surfaces appear,

oiled with sweet perfumery.

- the flowers nearby swoon gracefully.

THE SWAN

I

Andromache, I think of you! That false Simois
that narrow stream, meagre and sad, flowing there
where the immense majesty of your widowed grief,
shone out, growing from your tears,

stirred my fertile memory, suddenly,
as I was crossing the new Carrousel.
The old Paris is gone (the shape of a city
changes faster than the human heart can tell)

I can only see those frail booths in the mind's eye,
those piles of rough-cut pillars, and capitals,
the weeds, the massive greening blocks, that used to lie
water-stained: the bric-a-brac piled in shop windows.

There, there used to be a menagerie:
One dawn, at the hour when labour wakes, there,
under the cold, clear sky, or, when the road-menders set free
a dull hammering, into the silent air,

I saw a swan, that had escaped its cage,

striking the dry stones with webbed feet;

trailing, on hard earth, its white plumage;

in the waterless gutter, opening its beak;

bathing its wings frantically, in the dust,

and crying, its heart full of its native streams:

'Lightning, when will you strike? Rain when will you gust?'

Unfortunate, strange, fatal symbol, it seems

I see you, still: sometimes, like Ovid's true

man transformed, his head, on a convulsive neck, strained

towards the sky's cruel and ironic blue,

addressing the gods with his complaint.

II

Paris changes! But nothing, in my melancholy,

moves. New hotels, scaffolding, stone blocks,

old suburbs, everything, becomes allegory,

to me: my memories are heavier than rocks.

So, in front of the Louvre, an image oppresses me.

I think of my great swan, with its mad movements,

ridiculous, sublime, as exiles seem,

gnawed by endless longing! And then,

of you, Andromache, fallen from the embrace

of the great hero, vile chattel in the hands of proud Pyrrhus,

in front of an open tomb, in grief's ecstatic grace,

Hector's widow, alas, and wife of Helenus!

I think of the negress, consumptive, starved,

dragging through the mire, and searching, eyes fixed,

for the absent palm-trees of Africa, carved

behind the immense walls of mist:

Of those who have lost what they cannot recover,

ever! Ever! Those who drink tears like ours,

and suck on sorrow's breasts, their wolf-mother!

Of the skinny orphans, withering like flowers!

So in the forest of my heart's exile,

an old memory sounds its clear encore!

I think of sailors forgotten on some isle,

prisoners, the defeated! ....and of many more!

Note. Andromache was Hector's wife who mourned his death in the Trojan War. The Simois and the Scamander (Xanthus) were the two rivers of the Trojan Plain. Pyrrhus is Neoptolemus, son of Achilles. Andromache fell to him as a spoil after the fall of Troy. Helenus was a son of Priam and brother of Hector. Baudelaire follows Virgil, The Aeneid III 289, where Aeneas reaches Epirus and Chaonia, and finds Helenus and Andromache. Helenus has succeeded to the throne of Pyrrhus and married Andromache. Aeneas finds Andromache sacrificing to Hector's ashes in a wood near the city (Buthrotum) by a river named after the Simois. This is Baudelaire's 'false Simois'. Andromache explains that Pyrrhus has left her for Hermione, and passed her on to Helenus, who has been accepted as a Greek prince. Helenus has built a second 'little' Troy in Chaonia. Andromache is a symbol of fallen exile. The Carrousel is a bridge over the Seine in Paris, recent at the time of the poem. The Ovid reference is (arguably) to Cycnus, son of Sthenelus, changed to a swan, grieving for Phaethon (See Metamorphoses II 367 and also Virgil, Aeneid X 187). The Louvre Palace is now a Museum and Art Gallery, on the right bank of the Seine, in Paris.

PARISIAN DREAM

À Constantine Guys

I

The vague and distant image
of this landscape, so terrifying,
on which no mortal's gazed
thrilled me again this morning.

Sleep is full of miracles!
By a singular caprice
from that unfolding spectacle
I'd banned all shapeless leaf,

a painter proud of my artistry
I savoured in my picture
the enchanting monotony
of metal, marble, water.

Babel of stairs and arcades,

it was an infinite palace

full of pools and cascades,

falling gold, burnt, or lustreless:

and heavy cataracts there

like curtains of crystal,

dazzling, hung in air

from walls of metal.

Not trees, but colonnades

circled the sleeping pools

where colossal naiads gazed

at themselves, as women do.

Between banks of rose and green,

the blue water stretched,

for millions of leagues

to the universe's edge:

there were un-heard of stones,

and magic waves: there were,

dazzled by everything shown,

enormous quivering mirrors!

Impassive and taciturn,

Ganges, in the firmament,

poured treasures from the urn

into abysses of diamond.

Architect of this spell,

I made a tame ocean swell

entirely at my will,

through a jewelled tunnel:

and all, seemed glossy, clear

iridescent: even the shades

of black, liquid glory there

in light's crystallised rays.

Not a single star, no trace

of a sun even, low in the sky,

to illuminate this wondrous place

that shone with intrinsic fire!

And over these shifting wonders

hovered (oh dreadful novelty!

All for the eye, none for the ear!)

the silence of eternity.

II

Opening eyes filled with flame

I saw the horrors of my hovel,

and felt the barbs of shameful

care, re-entering my soul:

brutally with gloomy blows

the clock struck mid-day,

and the sky poured shadows

on a world, benumbed and grey.

THE INQUISITIVE MAN'S DREAM

Á Nadar

Do you know, as I do, delicious sadness
and make others say of you: 'Strange man!'
– I was dying. In my soul, singular illness,
desire and horror were mingled as one:

anguish and living hope, no factious bile.
The more the fatal sand ran out, the more
acute, delicious my torment: my heart entire
was tearing itself away from the world I saw.

I was like a child eager for the spectacle,
hating the curtain as one hates an obstacle...
at last the truth was chillingly revealed:

I'd died without surprise, dreadful morning
enveloped me. – Was this all there was to see?
The curtain had risen, and I was still waiting.

OBSESSION

Great forests you frighten me, like vast cathedrals:
You roar like an organ, and in our condemned souls,
aisles of eternal mourning, where past death-rattles
sound, the echo of your De Profundis rolls.

I hate you, Ocean! My mind, in your tumultuous main,
sees itself: I hear the vast laughter of your seas,
the bitter laughter of defeated men,
filled with the sound of sobs and blasphemies.

How you would please me without your stars, O Night!
I know the language that their light employs!
Since I search for darkness, nakedness, the Void!

But the shadows themselves seem, to my sight
canvases, where thousands of lost beings, alive,
and with a familiar gaze, leap from my eyes.

SYMPATHETIC HORROR

'From that sky livid, bizarre

as your tortured destiny,

what thoughts fill your empty heart,

Freethinker, answer me.'

— Insatiable and avid

for vague and obscure skies,

I'll not groan like Ovid,

banned from Rome and paradise.

Skies, shores split and seamed,

my pride's mirrored in you:

your clouds in mourning, too,

are the hearses of my dreams,

Hell's reflected in your light,

where my heart takes delight.

THE ALCHEMY OF SADNESS

One man lights you with his ardour

one decks you in mourning, Nature!

What says to the first: 'A Sepulchre!'

To the other cries: 'Life and splendour!'

Unknown Hermes, who assists,

yet intimidates me as well,

you make me Midas' equal,

the saddest of alchemists:

You help me change gold to iron,

paradise to hell's kingdom:

in the shrouded atmosphere

I find a dear corpse, and on

the celestial shores, it's there,

I build a mighty sepulchre.

Notes: Hermes was the mercurial Greek messenger god, spirit of alchemy, and as Hermes Trismegistes a source of wisdom. Midas was offered a gift by the god Bacchus, and asked to turn everything to gold. Bacchus reversed the dreadful results, at Midas' request.

DRAFT EPILOGUE
FOR THE SECOND EDITION OF LES FLEURS DU MAL

Tranquil as a sage and gentle as one who's cursed....I said:

I love you, oh my beauty, my charmer...

many a time...

your debauches without thirst, your soul-less loves,

your longing for the infinite

which proclaims itself everywhere, even in evil,

your bombs, knives, victory marches, public feasts,

your melancholy suburbs,

your furnished rooms,

your gardens full of sighs and intrigue,

your churches vomiting prayer as music,

your childish despairs, mad hags' games,

your discouragements:

and your fireworks, eruptions of joy,

that make the dumb and gloomy sky smile.

Your venerable vice dressed in silk,

and laughable virtue, with sad gaze,

gentle, delighting in the luxury it shows.

Your saved principles and flouted laws,

your proud monuments on which mists catch,

your metal domes the sun inflames,

your theatrical queens with seductive voices,

your tocsins, cannon, deafening orchestra,

your magic cobbles heaped as barricades,

your petty orators' swollen rhetoric,

preaching love, while your sewers run with blood,

rushing towards Hell like the Orinoco's flood,

your angels, your fresh clowns in ancient rags.

Angels dressed in gold, purple and hyacinth,

O you, bear witness that I've discharged my task,

like a perfect alchemist like a sainted soul.

From every thing I've extracted the quintessence,

you gave me your mud and I've turned it into gold.

EPILOGUE

With quiet heart, I climbed the hill,

from which one can see, the city, complete,

hospitals, brothels, purgatory, hell,

prison, where every sin flowers, at our feet.

You know well, Satan, patron of my distress,

I did not trudge up there to vainly weep,

but like an old man with an old mistress,

I longed to intoxicate myself, with the infernal delight

of the vast procuress, who can always make things fresh.

Whether you still sleep in the morning light,

heavy, dark, rheumatic, or whether your hands

flutter, in your pure, gold-edged veils of night,

I love you, infamous capital! Courtesans

and pimps, you often offer pleasures

the vulgar mob will never understand.

THE VOICE

I was the height of a folio, my bed just
backed on the bookcases' sombre Babel,
everything, Latin ashes, Greek dust
jumbled together: novel, science, fable.

Two voices spoke to me. One, firmly, slyly,
said: 'The Earth's a cake filled with sweetness:
I can give you (and your pleasure will be
endless!) an appetite of comparable vastness.'

The other said: 'Come! Come voyage in dream,
beyond the known, beyond the possible!'
And that one sang like the ocean breeze,
phantom, from who knows where, its wail

caressing the ear, and yet still frightening.
You I answered: 'Yes! Gentle voice!' My
wound, and what I'd call my fatality, begins
alas, from then. From behind the scenery

of vast existence, in voids without light,

I see the strangest worlds distinctly:

ecstatic victim of my second sight,

snakes follow me striking at my feet.

Since then, like the prophets, I greet

the desert and the sea with tenderness:

I laugh at funerals, I cry at feasts,

wine tastes smooth that's full of bitterness:

and, eyes on the sky, I fall into holes,

and frequently I take facts for lies.

But 'Keep your dreams!' the Voice consoles,

'Madmen have sweeter ones than the wise!'

THE WARNER

Every man worth the name
has a yellow snake in his soul,
seated as on a throne, saying
if he cries: 'I want to!': 'No!'

Lock eyes with the fixed gaze
of Nixies or Satyresses, says
the Tooth: 'Think of your duty!'

Make children, or plant trees,
polish verses, or marble frieze,
the Tooth says: 'Tonight, where will you be?'

Whatever he likes to consider
there's never a moment passing
a man can't hear the warning
of that insufferable Viper.

CALM

Have patience, O my sorrow, and be still.
You asked for night: it falls: it is here.
A shadowy atmosphere enshrouds the hill,
to some men bringing peace, to others care.

While the vile human multitude
goes to earn remorse, in servile pleasure's play,
under the lash of joy, the torturer, who
is pitiless, Sadness, come, far away:

Give me your hand. See, where the lost years
lean from the balcony in their outdated gear,
where regret, smiling, surges from the watery deeps.

Underneath some archway, the dying light
sleeps, and, like a long shroud trailing from the East,
listen, dear one, listen to the soft onset of night.

THE LID

Whatever place he goes, on land or sea,
under a sky on fire, or a polar sun,
servant of Jesus, follower of Cytherea,
shadowy beggar, or Croesus the glittering one,

city-dweller or rustic, traveller or sedentary,
whether his tiny brain works fast or slow,
everywhere man knows the terror of mystery,
and with a trembling eye looks high or low.

Above, the Sky! That burial vault that stifles,
a ceiling lit for a comic opera, blind walls,
where each actor treads a blood-drenched stage:

Freethinkers' fear, the hermit sets his hope on:
the Sky! The black lid of the giant cauldron,
under which we vast, invisible Beings rage.

THE SUNSET OF ROMANTICISM

How beautiful a new sun is when it rises,
flashing out its greeting, like an explosion!
– Happy, whoever hails with sweet emotion
its descent, nobler than a dream, to our eyes!

I remember! I've seen all, flower, furrow, fountain,
swoon beneath its look, like a throbbing heart…
– Let's run quickly, it's late, towards the horizon,
to catch at least one slanting ray as it departs!

But I pursue the vanishing God in vain:
irresistible Night establishes its sway,
full of shudders, black, dismal, cold:

an odour of the tomb floats in the shadow,
at the swamp's edge, feet faltering I go,
bruising damp slugs, and unexpected toads.

THE VOID

Pascal had his Void that went with him day and night.
- Alas! It's all Abyss, - action, longing, dream,
the Word! And I feel Panic's storm-wind stream
through my hair, and make it stand upright.

Above, below, around, the desert, the deep,
the silence, the fearful compelling spaces...
With his knowing hand, in my dark, God traces
a multi-formed nightmare without release.

I fear sleep as one fears a deep hole,
full of vague terror. Where to, who knows?
I see only infinity at every window,

and my spirit haunted by vertigo's stress
envies the stillness of Nothingness.
- Ah! Never to escape from Being and Number!

THE MOON, OFFENDED

Oh moon our fathers worshipped, their love discreet,

from the blue country's heights where the bright seraglio,

the stars in their sweet dress, go treading after you,

my ancient Cynthia, lamp of my retreat,

do you see the lovers, in their bed's happiness

showing in sleep their mouths' cool enamels,

the poet bruising his forehead on his troubles,

or the vipers coupling under the dry grass?

Under your yellow cloak, with clandestine pacing,

do you pass as before, from twilight to morning,

to kiss Endymion's faded grace?

- 'I see your mother, Child of this impoverished century,

who, over her mirror, bends a time-worn face,

and powders the breast that fed you, skilfully.'

LAMENT OF AN ICARUS

Lovers of whores don't care,
happy, calm and replete:
But my arms are incomplete,
grasping the empty air.

Thanks to stars, incomparable ones,
that blaze in the depths of the skies,
all my destroyed eyes
see, are the memories of suns.

I look, in vain, for beginning and end
of the heavens' slow revolve:
Under an unknown eye of fire, I ascend
feeling my wings dissolve.

And, scorched by desire for the beautiful,
I will not know the bliss,
of giving my name to that abyss,
that knows my tomb and funeral.

VOYAGE TO MODERNITY

A new commentary on Baudelaire's poetry

'Ostende' – Félicien Rops (Belgian, 1833 – 1898)
LACMA Collections

Voyage to Modernity presents a new critical interpretation of Baudelaire's poetry, supported and illustrated by the preceding translations of eighty-eight of the major poems from his collection *Les Fleurs du mal*. The study champions Baudelaire as the first major writer to highlight the schisms in the human psyche created by modernity; that mix of secular thought, social transformation, and self-reflective awareness that characterises life in the post-Enlightenment, and predominantly urban, world.

The study concentrates on key modern divisions explored and expressed by Baudelaire in his life and his verse, for example those between humanity and nature, the city and the individual, and between the sexes. As well as highlighting the recurrent themes, symbols and images of his art, and his largely unacknowledged debt to Dante, this critical approach portrays Baudelaire as a profound moralist in a long tradition, and far from the superficial immoralist he was portrayed as in his own day. It again lays claim to him as the progenitor of modern intellectual poetry, while restating his vital significance in the history of thought, as well as communicating the profundity and beauty of his enduring art.

I: INTRODUCTION: THE INVITATION TO THE VOYAGE

Romanticism begins and ends in the Idyll: a voyage from cradle to cradle, from dream to exhausted calm. Romanticism: dissatisfied with its own perpetually thwarted emotions, wearied with the imperfect and frustrating reality. Romanticism: searching for what cannot be found on Earth or in the sky. So the Romantic Mind attempts to construct its own versions of paradise: artificial and delicate of construction, fragile and doomed by time and death, by emotional erosion and internal frailties. So Mind returns, through nostalgia and the evocation of memory, through dream and drug-induced trance, through contemplation and reverie, to its first enchantments: and embraces, with sensitivity and anxiety, the last music of its hard-won artistic creation. Baudelaire, above all, knew and loved Romanticism's dream, its '*goût de l'infini*', its longing for the infinite, Baudelaire who gave his life, as he claimed, to the creation of *gold from mud* [p. 155], Baudelaire who struck glittering nails into Romanticism's coffin, even as he mused on its glorious but short-lived existence, a poet who pursued in vain the departing *god* [p. 163].

Baudelaire learnt from Dante. The Earthly Paradise, since there is no heavenly one for the adult mind, is entered into, if anywhere, from the summit of the Mount of Purgatory, after the long hard climb. There if anywhere is the gateway to a higher state of being. There the Romantics, and all of us, must go in search: and if the Earthly Paradise is not to be found, if there is no Mount except in the human mind, if where we are is more akin to the Inferno, then mind itself must create its own mountain, fashion its own wings, plant its own Garden, re-win its lost innocence, invoke the Idyll.

'Dante et Virgile aux Enfers' – Eugène Delacroix (French, 1798 – 1863)
The Yorck Project: 10.000 Meisterwerke der Malerei, 2002
Directmedia Publishing GmbH – *Wikimedia Commons*

Baudelaire is a Dante in whom the Vision fades, for whom the *Paradiso* is no more than a distant passing gleam, a spirit who has fallen, with Satan the Angel of Pride, into the pit, *le gouffre*, and must wind his way to Satan's presence, climb that monster's shaggy hide in reverse, and then begin the toil of ascending the slope of the self-created Mount but without faith or hope, with no Virgil as companion to lead him to Beatrice. It is a journey of the heart and spirit: it is the voyage of a Ulysses past un-fortunate Isles, the journey of a pilgrim, the stumbling steps of the Individual, under the glare of History, and then no History. It is an endless setting sail, but not towards Byzantium. Here, in Hell, even in the crowd, especially in the crowd, we are alone. Hell is a place where we can go neither forward nor back, where language is corrupted by the swarm, where the voices and cries fail to communicate anything but their madness or pain, where community is lost, and nothing can be given while all must be taken.

Baudelaire read Dante. And he too is a Classicist: that is an artist who sets his work within the context of symbols derived from past art, and for whom art itself is a means of knowledge and self-justification, beyond mere entertainment. He is a traditionalist too in that his great concern is with the moral centre, with the question of how to live, how to be, in a universe that reveals itself as ultimately intention-less and without recourse. In his hands the mud of despair must somehow be fashioned, through art's alchemy, into the gold of poetry, the mud of the abyss must somehow become the clear water and green fields of the Idyll, of the childhood paradise, but he is a Romantic first of all, one who has nothing but his own mind and spirit to begin with, and a Modern, perhaps the first true Modern, who has nothing but his own mind and spirit to end with also.

Unlike Dante, Baudelaire is denied an ascent. The old certainties evaporate. It is pointless to claim Baudelaire as a lapsed believer, as a seeker after the faith, temporarily separated from it. What does he himself say, late on in his life (Rockets XXII) 'As for religion I consider it useless to speak of it, or to search for any remains of it, since in such matters the only thing that nowadays gives rise to scandal is to take the trouble to deny God.' He may have despised the casual indifference of the freethinkers to faith, his own life may have ended in some kind of ironic Catholicism, but if so, that was a weakness, a failure, not the success of his life. His heart and his mind do not believe, despite his great longing for the lost paradise, the lost solace of the religion of his childhood. His poetry is modern precisely because it rejects that for which there is no evidence. And so, for Baudelaire's art, in this life there are only the worlds of one's own creation, never the Empyrean created by another. And ultimately he does not even believe in his own Satan. Earth is not, for him, ruled by some divine manifestation of evil, rather it is a landscape devoid of all divine or satanic meaning. The paradise we long for is not tangible anywhere, the fall we experience is from the flight of our own making for which we finally lack the strength, evil is mere banal repetition, an obsession, an addiction, and purgatory, which is a repetition in the mind of the inferno of actuality, leads not to salvation and paradise but at best to an embittered or exhausted quietude.

If we cannot ascend, we are forced instead (given that we refuse to merely sit still and accept) to make our rounds of the world, the universe, in which we find ourselves. Life and thought is therefore Voyage, Baudelaire's deepest symbol, the one to which all his poetry returns, since poetry itself, each poem, is in itself a voyage towards a known or unknown creative harbour, and because many of his greatest poems are poems explicitly about voyaging, 'from the *dark sea* [p. 112] of the sordid city, towards another sea, a blaze of splendour that is blue, bright, deep as virginity', towards 'that sea which is the Infinite', 'somewhere out of this world'.

There are many impulses to the voyage, but a deep Romantic restlessness is in Baudelaire the most powerful and 'the true voyagers [p. 127] are those who leave only to move', those who give themselves to the winds and the waves, like the great sea-birds or the swans, the voyagers of the sky, like *Icarus* [p. 166] on the wings that Daedalus made for him, those who fly and are doomed to fall. There are other voyagers too, those Classical travellers, driven by circumstance, Ulysses or Orestes or Aeneas, who are referred to indirectly in the verse, but they are less powerful images for him. His true travellers have no destination other than that evoked by their own dreams and fantasies. They voyage 'Into the *Unknown's depths* [p. 127], to find the *new*.' The word 'Unknown' emerges as a frequently repeated key to his poetry. They are travelling beyond the accepted and familiar, into whatever can relieve the pain and monotony of an existence that offers no hope and no salvation. And the Reader must accept the Invitation to the Voyage, just as the beloved he addresses must, as we all must. The Invitation to the Voyage is also the invitation to the Idyll, to the pursuit of the Idyll, the pursuit of paradise, whether it is the paradise of the indolent Lotus Eaters, or the paradise of the dream, whether it is the paradise of the doomed lovers, or the paradise of the ocean calm, or that of the moonlit night when the weary soul achieves momentary rest.

What else does Baudelaire take from Dante? His vision of Hell, yes: but more importantly his moral centre. No vision of the Inferno, such as Dante and Baudelaire possess, is meaningful without extreme sensitivity to pain, to harm, to deathliness, to betrayal, to personal failing, pride, lust, to all the sins and vices, anxieties and fevers. Baudelaire's hell lacks the feeling of divine retribution and punishment that Dante's expresses, it is a hell of reality, a hell of the human condition, imposed perhaps, or accidental perhaps, but not infused with divine meaning. If Baudelaire too is a Catholic, he is an immensely strange one. Yet the moral centre is clear. All Baudelaire's Satanism, his flowers of evil, his toying with vice, sin, the consciousness of the infamous, are trappings, never his essence. His essence is always the search for incorruptible love, for true meaning, for an endless ecstasy of feeling and sensation, for a world of delight that does not exist for us except momentarily, for solace and consolation, for a defence against time, mortality, betrayal, and disappointment.

His sinners are searchers, fleeing from *ennui*, that spiritual malaise of the superfluous man, fleeing through sin towards the unknown, gripped by fever, tormented by remorse, but forever pure in their vices, forever human as we are. The harm his sinners perpetrate is primarily against the self. Violence, the corruption of others, deliberate offences against our fellow creatures' spirits, those are aspects of a De Sade, not a Baudelaire. Baudelaire's sinners are caught in the meshes of obsession and infatuation, their vices are repetitions, almost a definition of sin for Baudelaire as it was for Goethe 'that which we cannot stop doing', that which we cannot evade. His sinners are gamblers, petty criminals, faithless whores, self-tormenters, sexual deviants, religious flagellants those who are always trying to satisfy a deeper restlessness through the mechanisms of a surface anxiety or addiction. And they are those with whom we have empathy, because they are, as we are, says Baudelaire, in search of an artificial paradise, a haven, a harbour, blessed by Venus, or Fortuna, by '*Madonna* [p. 108], Muse or Guardian Angel.'

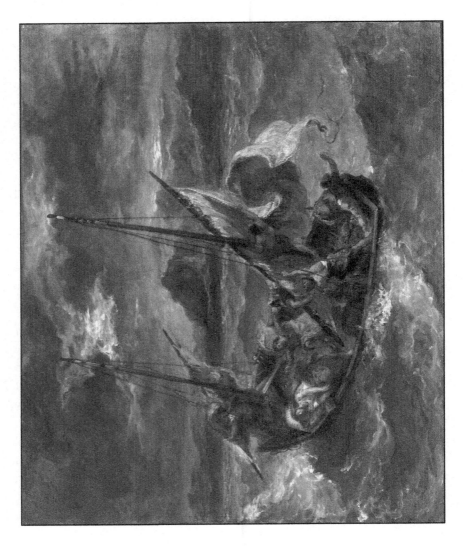

'Christ sur la Mer de Galilée' - Eugène Delacroix (French, 1798 - 1863)
Walters Art Musuem - *Wikimedia Commons*

Baudelaire's hell is Dante's without its rationale. But the moral dilemma, and agony, is as valid, even more so. Is there a true equivalent of Dante's Purgatory in Baudelaire's writing? To answer that we must revisit Dante's concept of the universe founded on relationship. His hell is where relationship fails, in the great betrayal and denial of faith, truth, hope, and love. His Purgatory is then a realm where relationship is re-established, where language, fractured, guttural and destructive in the Inferno, is purified and becomes a vehicle of hope. And is not relationship Baudelaire's fundamental problem, how to achieve relationship, how to preserve it against time and fate, how to understand the relationship between the individual and society, the individual and Nature, how to relate? Because Baudelaire, that hyper-sensitive child was damaged by a close, and subsequently fractured, to him betrayed, relationship with his mother? Because fruitful relationship with women was his great desire, despite his often misogynistic condemnation of Woman, but achieved in only swift flashes of light between periods of darkness? Because, more profoundly for his art, the old relationship with deity, nature and society was broken in his time, and the reality of the human situation flooded in upon us, our spiritual isolation as a species and therefore our loneliness, our separation through consciousness and culture from the nature that spawned us and partially defines us, and our mechanisation of society, the re-definition of work and home, individuality and purpose that the modern industrialised, urbanised world has forced upon us? Baudelaire's purgatory is this life also, overlapping with his hell. It is the mind re-working its experience in an effort to understand and transmute the real. It is therefore like hell itself a repetition, only this time in the realm of thought and feeling, of the fundamental pain of existence, and its torments are no less severe than the experience of hell itself.

There are reasons for Baudelaire's alienation from his world, and his search for other worlds, that are attributable to his private life, his childhood, his sensibility. But they are only the pre-dispositions that enable his art and thought: they do not in any way determine or exhaust them. When a world-shattering change takes place in society, intellectual life, and spirituality, a fracturing of old values and old relationships, then it should be no surprise if it is those individuals whose temperament, intellect and early life mirrors aspects of that change, and sensitises them to it, who are most likely to take up the task of understanding and confronting it. But if

Baudelaire's mind had not mirrored what was happening beyond and outside him, then his art would only be of interest to specialists, or to his biographers, not to us all. Likewise, nothing in Dante's life 'explains' Dante in a reductionist sense, but many elements of it go to produce the kind of mind and experience out of which his art emerged.

What else does Baudelaire take from Dante? He takes his sense of destiny, of history, of being at the focal point of a new sensibility, his sense of individuality. Dante is his own protagonist as Baudelaire is, as all profound modern creators are. Dante blends history with mythology, present with past, in the living moment. So does Baudelaire. The Individual, humble, even humiliated, travels forward, as hero or anti-hero, and makes a journey through the universe. Dante's life, his love, his feelings, his form, goes out into the voyage through the three realms, as 'one alone'. So does Baudelaire, who sees his own age more clearly, lives it more intensely, and analyses it more fiercely than others. Baudelaire is a supreme individual, as Dante is, and so curiously they become archetypal. No one else lives their lives, or even feels exactly as they do, but they give out the tocsin sound of their age, and send its echoes, resonating, across the streets and fields, across the earth and sea, into the furthest depths of their time. Baudelaire is even more his own voyager than Dante, his own traveller, identifying with all voyagers, all vessels, all wanderers, all exiles, all passers-by, everything that moves, sails, swims, flies, and falls. He attempts the heroic, even though the chances of success in such a world as ours are negligible. The heroic age is past, and yet, he contends, there is heroism in modern life, in facing it squarely, with clarity and courage, with that intellect and full awareness that Baudelaire sought to celebrate.

Baudelaire, without a comprehensive system, nevertheless explores his universe, as Dante explores his system: he watches, waits, listens, longs, hopes, as Dante does. But Baudelaire's labours can at best aim for some vision of that Earthly Paradise at the top of the Mount of Purgatory, an Earthly Paradise in whose permanence and recovery he hardly believes. So hope is matched by despair, faith is elusive at best, charity often withheld, and love and relationship are fragile, dangerous, and fraught with harm and hurt.

Paradise flees from us, leaving behind its fragments, poems, memories, those feelings and sensations locked within us that can be evoked, re-evoked. For the Classical poet, this world was enough: this world that Greece and Rome celebrate, a world incorporating its gods, not divorced from them. For the Medieval poet the other world was real, and Dante and Petrarch celebrate its reality and its impact on this world. But for the Romantics and for Modernity, this world is never enough, and the paradise that we dream is irretrievably lost, never to be recovered beyond and outside us, only within us, since no external power exists that can restore it, nor are we great enough to create it externally ourselves. Baudelaire, like Shelley, is one of the first great poets of that loss, that isolation, that realisation. It is a realisation that many of us, most perhaps, shy away from. It can itself seem a flower of evil. But to those who are aware in the fully Modern sense, then it is also our reality, and of it we must make what we can.

What more does Baudelaire take from Dante? He takes his vision of hell as a city, the city as hell. For Baudelaire that involves its varied aspects of humanity crammed into a tiny space, its panoply of human behaviour, its existence almost as a living being in its own right, a seething ant-heap, its potential callousness, indifference, insanity, its juxtaposition of human states, its conflict of extremes, wealth with poverty, beauty with ugliness, truth with deceit, kindness with crime, love with hatred. The city is humanity objectified, made the instrument of the market, all the markets where we buy and sell things and ourselves. The city is an ogre, a monster, but also a thing of veils and enchantments, a seductive whore, a theatre, a landscape of arcades and canals, buildings and streets, vehicles and passers-by. Because there is no Mount of Purgatory and no Paradise for Baudelaire except the artificial paradises of his imagination, then the city is, more potently, Hell. There is no City of the Church, no City of God, only the city of Mankind, of Reality. Those relationships that do exist he views within its context. Escape from the city, to search for new possibilities, hopes of relationship, can only be by a voyage of mind or body, even though all voyages disappoint, except perhaps (a vague and unreal one perhaps) the last voyage with Captain Death. The city of hell is Paris in reality, as for Dante it was Florence transposed. But not only are all the sins and vices of hell there, so is the flattened purgatory, the collapsed mountain, because after all in purgatory Dante says that we re-visit the sins of hell in expiation, and what difference is there in Baudelaire's essentially godless world between suffering the sin, and suffering it again in repetition, in thought, in remorse, in purgation?

Dante's world is full of political resonance, Baudelaire's it might seem is not. Where in his city is Dante's war of factions, his dream of a separated Church and State, the struggle for a return to order, both divine and imperial? Baudelaire is seemingly apolitical. Yet he takes the stance of the non-conformist, he focuses on the private and individual, on sexuality, vice, addiction, dream, on everything that fills the vacuum of days. On the one hand he opposes that meaningless work that the city can exemplify, from which we run for relief to vanities, to personal space: on the other he celebrates true work, the work of the mind even while he despairs of its limitations. He is in the one mode a celebrator, in words, of the strange beauty of the desolate landscape of modernity, on the other an opponent of its objectification, its ruthlessness, its coldness.

In Baudelaire, unlike Dante, politics becomes separated from human aspiration. It is an aspect of the 'failed' Revolution, that of the spirit. Political activity is relegated, perhaps for the first time in Baudelaire, to its position of controlling the public mechanisms of our lives, unable in modernity to satisfy our inner aspirations other than momentarily, but whose glitter like a firework, a jewel, a beautiful woman, occupies us, attracts our eyes, and deceives us for a while. Modern politics wields power, but as part of a process with little linkage to the realities of our inner beings. And yet we have long-ago passed beyond primitivism: and the charms of the native and the natural, like the charms of the exotic for Baudelaire, ultimately disappoint. The natives are prone to reveal the same stink, the same immorality, and the same addiction to false gods as we civilised ones betray. There is no way back. That is Baudelaire's message. There is no way back, only a voyage on into the unknown, if we can find a new unknown to sail towards. So Baudelaire is not possessed as Dante was by political aspiration, and his 'political' dimension is precisely that rejection of politics as a means to redemption that its absence in his poetry proclaims. There are no public Utopias at the end of Baudelaire's tunnels. His paradises are not practicalities, because he knows them to be ultimately unreal.

What else does Baudelaire take from Dante? He takes his vision of Beatrice, of the Ideal beloved, though he cannot import her embodiment or realisation into his world. He can meet her for an instant in purgatory but not be led by her to 'paradise', at least not for more than a moment. The purgatorial voyage towards Beatrice over 'a sea less cruel' in Dante's universe, is, in Baudelaire's, a Voyage to *Cythera* [p. 74], to ultimate self-disgust. Yet Baudelaire is a love poet in the deepest sense, in that love, or rather relationship, of which love is the supreme example, is his main theme, his main desire, the object of his primary search, and its lack the reason for his most profound disappointment. It is because he searches for and fails to find an analogue for love and relationship in external reality that he is a modern. It is because the real world fails us in our deepest longing, for ultimate and permanent contact, and not simply because his own insecurities sensitised him to that failure, that Baudelaire is important to us. The Voyage to which he invites us is also our voyage towards Cythera, Venus, and the Ideal.

I here consider his poetry under six main headings, while acknowledging that the themes treated within each are inextricably interwoven with the others. Baudelaire does not set out to be a systematic thinker, a system-builder, he is a witness: his poetry a reaction to his age. So he approaches the same ideas and symbolic meanings from many different directions, and can carry within himself contradictions, unresolved dilemmas, the love combined with hate that is an aspect of our own inner complexity and the complexity of the world it mirrors.

Firstly there is the Vision of Paradise or of the Idyllic that is the deepest impulse in Baudelaire. The real world fails to satisfy, fails to be an arena in which intense permanent relationship can be established, fails to fully engage the intellect imbued with deep feeling, and that lack of engagement engenders spiritual weariness, *ennui*. We counter *ennui* by the construction of artificial paradises, by setting out towards the mirages of new virgin paradises, or by attempting to regain those we believe we have lost. Baudelaire's art reveals many such journeys and attempts.

'Port de Bordeaux' – Édouard Manet (French, 1832 – 1883)
The Yorck Project: 10.000 Meisterwerke der Malerei, 2002
Directmedia Publishing GmbH – *Wikimedia Commons*

Secondly there is the Vision of Venus Cytherea, of Ideal Love and its corrupted refractions, of Woman, the potential source of the deepest relationship for the heterosexual male, with Woman as mother, lover, sister, daughter, companion, or an erotic and spiritual mixture of all five. Baudelaire, in tune with his times, but also partially conditioned by his early experiences, is one of those whose view of Woman is frequently polarised, seeing her either as cool, inflexible, superior to man, the chaste Madonna and Ideal Beauty, or as sensual witch, the potential betrayer. Either dimension can itself polarise into refuge or place of torment. As temporary refuge Woman is an aspect of the Idyll, an aspect like Beatrice in Dante's art and life of Paradise itself, though here a fragile and momentary one. As tormentor, Woman is an aspect of hell, as in Dante's Purgatorial dream of the Siren. She is then the voice and symbol of unreason and unfaith. Yet Baudelaire sees Woman too in other aspects between the poles, and all the dimensions of his search for relationship with the sex need to be considered.

Thirdly there is the Vision of Hell itself as exemplified in the City. Hell is the crowd, the seethe of experience, the roaring ocean of the illusory *samsara*, the wind and wave of a new kind of sea exemplified by nineteenth century Paris, the great urban metropolis, a monster, an *ogre* [p. 136], swallowing and consuming, filled with savage frenzy, an emblem of the meaningless heave and swell of modern existence, where the Individual may be isolated, exiled and divorced from true relationship. Yet the city too has other aspects, it has its solitudes, its silences: hell too has its charms! If we voyage to escape the crowd, the city of Dis, then the voyage itself returns us to its harbour, what Baudelaire called 'the intersection of its myriad relations'.

Fourthly there is the Voyage itself, the great voyage to which his poetry invites us, of thought and feeling, around the world which becomes Modernity, the world of limitation. The dreams of paradise fall apart, the vision of Woman fails to establish the kind of eternal relationship demanded and desired, the city of hell corrupts our sensibilities and dulls our being, Satan palls, and we are without a god, or possessed of a god so remote and dubious, so potentially inimical to existence, that reality becomes the Void. The Voyage into the Void is the Voyage to Modernity.

Fifthly there is its impact on the poet, on the individual human being: there is the self-image created, the awareness of self which results. Baudelaire begins with the attempt to make the poet his own hero, as Dante does, but the 'heroism of modern life' demands an effort beyond the abilities of the greatest. How can one mind embrace the multitude, when all is equally valid? Nevertheless the modern mind's attempt to grasp its world entire is heroic, just as the failure of that attempt is heroic. Does the failure of that effort make a failure of the life? Then we are all failures in modernity, and it is the relative success, the relative achievement that defines us. Perhaps even heroism is no longer the right mode in which to approach reality. Perhaps the failure of heroism is also the failure of Western Civilisation and of all civilisation to provide a means by which its participants can truly come to terms with life in all its absurdity (and not by falsely adopting some exploded myth of the past, with its gods and demons, or some false pseudo-science long superseded). Perhaps in fact Civilisation is a process and not a progress, a context and not an end, richness and not resolution.

Finally we can assess the Vision of Calm that Baudelaire achieves at times in his verse, rarely, but infinitely sweetly when it is achieved. Is it reply or evasion, satisfaction or exhaustion? He finds harbour, and is rocked to rest there. He is carried to the shore of his own sea of thought and activity. Near the end of his creative journey he has glimpses of peace, and even slides ironically, in his weakness, towards the embrace of a devalued religion he desires, but no longer believes in.

Baudelaire's art, and more than that his life, is an Invitation to the Voyage, to the Voyage that ended in Modernity. And are we beyond Modernity? That remains to be seen.

II: THE IDYLL (THE VISION OF PARADISE)

The search for the Idyll is ultimately the search for a miracle by which mortality can be overcome: mortality not just of the flesh, our finite lives, but of all experience. Everything 'action [p. 164], longing, dream, the Word' vanishes into oblivion second by second. Who of us has not longed to freeze and hold the moment of transitory pleasure, knowing it will pass? Who has not found the impossibility of doing so, since to live we must really live, not merely imagine ourselves living. In living we cannot observe the moment in all its richness, while in observing we cannot live the essential experience. The desire to catch mortality fleeing is the essence of voyeurism, the sensation that by watching we can capture what it means to experience, since in experiencing we cannot see ourselves vanishing, only feel the flight of time.

And the flight of time is our ultimate tragedy. That is Mephistopheles claim in Goethe's Faust (Part II, line 11600), 'Past, and pure nothing, complete monotony! What use is this eternal creation! Creating, to achieve annihilation! "There, it's past!" What's to read in it? It's just the same as if it never lived, yet chases round in circles, as if it did. I'd prefer to have the everlasting void.' All passes, all vanishes, nothing has permanent value. Firstly the childhood paradise is taken from us, snatched away, as it was from Baudelaire, or so his inner self believed. Then we search to replace it, through love, through action, through dream, through work, through pleasure, through intoxication and trance, through belief, through (above all, and in all these modes) the search for relationship with something outside us that can be relied on, something that roots the self in eternity, floats us above the Void, and creates a harbour where we can return, a spiritual home where we are recognised and can be at peace, we voyagers on the surface of the infinite. Given the lack of the Earthly Paradise, the impossibility of return to it, and through it return to the greater Paradise, we are left to search for what we can. We should examine Baudelaire's options, because they are also ours.

With memories of his 1841 voyage to Mauritius present in his mind, he holds out for us in his early poetry the possibilities of the exotic as a destination, the seductive dream of some land of pleasure where we will be rocked to sleep in the balm-laden atmosphere of a distant isle, an island of Circe or Calypso, or a shore of the Lotus-eaters, all images from the Odyssey that explicitly or implicitly emerge in his verse. It is 'a *perfumed* [p. 14] land caressed by the sun', 'a shore of *bliss* [p. 56]' an 'infinite *lullaby* [p. 57], full of the balm of leisure' a land 'where *luxury* [p. 85] delights in reflecting itself as order: where life is full and sweet to breathe: from which disorder, turbulence, the unforeseen are banished: where happiness is married to silence:' Intoxicated there, the spirit is caressed not just by the dream climate, but by the presence of the beloved (unmarred by her reality) that other great destination, Woman. The unfortunate are already exiled from such a delightful far country, they are like the woman of *Malabar* [p. 15], or the consumptive negress of The *Swan* [p. 143], struggling through the hell of the city, selling their charms in the sullen market of Capitalism. Freedom has become commodity. This imagined woman, exiled, traces of her black ancestry evident, and corresponding to the Jeanne Duval of Baudelaire's own life, is a prostituted equivalent, a Parisian shadow, of Gauguin's exotic Eve. She is fallen from every paradise, but precious to Baudelaire for that reason.

The exotic is a means of escape from the real. We love to journey through the countries of our imagination. But later we will find the falseness of our vision of those lands, the enchanted isle is only the isle of *Icarus* [p. 127] the fallen one, a barren reef, and not the Eldorado promised by destiny, or it is the terrible island of *Cythera* [p. 74], of self-disgust, dark and sad, no longer the golden land. Two great poems, Voyage to *Cythera* [p. 74] and The *Voyage* [p. 127], are Baudelaire's farewell to the dream islands, so that even when he revisits them in his verse again, they are forever lost. The imagery of the voyage enriches his poetry immeasurably, but in the end it is one more series of phantasms, one more elusive veil drawn over the face of our reality.

'Ovide chez les Scythes' – Eugène Delacroix (French, 1798 – 1863)
The Yorck Project: 10.000 Meisterwerke der Malerei, 2002
Directmedia Publishing GmbH – *Wikimedia Commons*

Behind the dream island, the enchanted space, lie our memories of childhood, the good memories not the terrors, where innocence plays in a land of plenty, and where beauty is at our command with all its freshness, as yet unrecognised and so a gift not understood, but preserved until later. Baudelaire evokes that world, whose retrieval is in the hands of memory. In his earliest verse he combines the dream of the exotic with this attempt to recapture the '*young loves* [p. 10], God gives, at the start of our lives'. And again the dream of a 'far, perfumed paradise' immediately invokes 'the green paradise of childhood's thrill' in *Moesta et Errabunda* [p. 112]. Yet Baudelaire writes little about childhood, perhaps because it was too lost a continent, too painful in its associations for him. One clear poem of memory recalls the *white house* [p. 19] of childhood (at Neuilly in 1827), near to the town, but there is an ominous undercurrent in the poem, and the staring eye of the sun, 'a huge eye in a curious heaven' is perhaps doomed to be the stepfather's eye, the eye of the cold god of inspectors and generals, rather than a loving eye. And remembering Mariette, his old nurse, the 'great-hearted *servant* [p. 20]' now dead, only serves to contrast the past with the present, and speak of spoiled promise, abandoned hopes.

Woman is a potential paradise. Already Baudelaire has coupled the exotic landscape with the erotic woman. This is Woman as object, the strange and quasi-mythological primitive, or the subject of a fetishist commoditisation, her *hair* [p. 57], her *fragrance* [p. 56] an opportunity to invoke the Idyll, to drown in the sea of her body, to conjure, as Proust learned, *memory* [p. 59] from the senses, or to sink deep into the enchanted spell of her *eyes* [p. 18], those other oceans that open not onto Mind, but onto forgetfulness, languor, the embrace of mystery, Night. All these oceans offer a voyage into temporary paradise, all these seas: cloud, darkness, eyes, hair, *memory* [p. 54] and childhood, where mother and lover are combined, in the sensual waves where new suns might rise.

'La Grèce sur les Ruines de Missolonghi'
Eugène Delacroix (French, 1798 – 1863)
The Yorck Project: 10.000 Meisterwerke der Malerei, 2002
Directmedia Publishing GmbH – *Wikimedia Commons*

These images are not so much realities, landscapes, women, objects, as atmospheres, media, contexts, for the creation of the Idyll. They are places where we can submerge, like the mother's dress that the child hugs, they are places of escape, and Baudelaire knows it. After all we have much to escape from. All forms of escape are potential landscapes for the Idyll: they are all potential artificial paradises. So in The Poem of Hashish, in his prose work Paradise by Artifice, Baudelaire offers drugs as a source of escape, preferable to liquor in creating what he calls the 'artificial Ideal'. The *Voyage* [p. 127] later calls them the 'least stupid' option. We should not however be deceived into considering Baudelaire an addict. He was too mistrustful of all infatuations and addictions to commit to anything that destroyed his ability to create, and the Poem of Hashish as it progresses turns into an indictment of the after-effects, as they appear in *Parisian* [p. 147] Dream, of drug-induced hallucination, and of the drugs themselves as forms of slow suicide. Above all Baudelaire condemns their moral effect, the enslavement of the addict, the stimulation of the imagination coupled with a weakening of the will that destroys any benefit accrued. 'One must always be drunk', he proclaimed in a prose poem, 'but with what? With wine, poetry, or virtue': very respectable, time-honoured options.

Remote exotic islands, erotic objectified women, drugs, memories, as an escape from the claustrophobia of pain and mortal sensation, as for example in the poem *Harmony* [p. 114] of Evening: all the landscapes of paradise: Baudelaire searches always for the possibilities: had not the *Voice* [p. 158] whispered to him, seduced him, had he not chosen? *Correspondences* [p. 43] is a poem that suggests that all sensations can be symbolic means of arousing ecstasy, especially perfumes, odours, fragrances, scents. *Landscape* [p. 22] shows Baudelaire relying on imagination and the power of the artist's will alone, lifted beyond the mundane, far from the crowd, and this concept of upwards flight he often employs. Flight is at the heart of poems like *Incompatibility* [p. 12] where the Idyll is muted and ambiguous, *Elevation* [p. 41] which echoes Correspondences in celebrating thought linked to the depths of the objective world seen as symbolic, and *Lover's Wine* [p. 121] with its suggestion of sensual, sexual ecstasy as a flight from the tormented world.

What more? Vice, infatuation, lust, avarice, gaming, the darkness of the city, its underworld, they are all means of escape for the masses, but Baudelaire himself does not suggest the many forms of self-indulgence, sin and addiction as true gateways to any even temporarily substantial paradise. They are a sad consequence of our moral corruption and of our search for the false Idyll, and they lead to self-disgust. That will become more obvious as we focus later on Baudelaire's understanding of modernity itself. His moral power derives from his deep inner moral outrage at what we do to ourselves as human beings, and the city is the landscape in which he addresses the less savoury means of escape from the self. But total escape from the self is not the Idyll. Paradise is not achieved by self-forgetting, only by extreme self-awareness, or it is merely a false freedom. Baudelaire's attempts at discovering paradise through voyage, Woman, flight, submersion in obsession, while frequently sensual in ambience, are not swoons. They are entries into heightened worlds, where perception is deeper, stranger, richer. And they can be transferred to paper, endowed with vitality. 'Out of nature has been distilled fantasy' he states in The Painter of Modern Life.

And when all voyages seem exhausted is there perhaps one more. Perhaps at the end the gates will open, and the angel will appear, as in The *Death of Lovers* [p. 63], the miraculous inn will be filled with light as in The *Death of the Poor* [p. 71], and we will sail on with Captain Death into the unknown, into a further *voyage* [p. 127].

The idea of the Idyll, of the distant paradise, is ever-present in Baudelaire's poems. And if that were all that there was to his life-work, if he had only written poems that encapsulate the Idyll, as a possibly attainable Ideal, then he would remain for us a late-Romantic, chasing Keats' nightingale, or Shelley's enchanted isles. It is his ruthless, clear-eyed vision of the modern reality around him that prevented him remaining in that situation, that made him pass on beyond Coleridge's Abyssinian Maid, to a harsher, fiercer contemplation. Part of that clarity, ruthlessness and harshness, stems from his view of Woman, and his failure to find in relationship with the other sex, as in his relationship with the external world, a permanently consoling resolution of his frustrations.

III: VOYAGE TO CYTHERA (THE VISION OF VENUS)

In The Painter of Modern Life (X), Baudelaire calls Woman an Idol, a kind of enchantress, 'the source of the most vivid and also...most lasting delights.' And yet in his last Brussels notebooks he calls her 'simultaneously the sin and the Hell that punishes it.' Does he love Woman or hate her? The answer is both. Perhaps the root of his attitude lies in that relationship with his mother, Caroline, at first idyllic, then shattered, betrayed and compromised in Baudelaire's terms, by her re-marriage, and ultimately soured and saddened by their tensions over money, and her lack of deep understanding of his needs and his art. However it is facile to try and interpret the power of Baudelaire's poetry in terms of one relationship: that with his mother. While he plays out the drama of that relationship internally, and in his letters to her, while the 'betrayal' of that relationship sensitised him to the potential failure of all relationship, the potential for betrayal always implicit in intense, even excessive, love, that refuses to accept anything less than the Ideal, it also led him towards an adult, not merely an infantile, truth of existence, that all things pass, all is mortal, all that we most rely on is evanescent and liable to 'betray' us.

It does not require us to rake over the ashes of his relationship with his mother, for us to be in tune with the disasters of relationship that lurk around us, and that are always in tension with our desire for a perfect love, a deeper paradise, an achieved Ideal, a lasting and unshakeable relationship, where we are always forgiven, and always inspired to exercise our greatest and most creative powers. Baudelaire's view of Woman is not unusual for its time. And perhaps the deeper source of his attitude is precisely the refusal to treat woman as an equal, an attitude common to his age, but rather to objectify Woman in her archetypal, mythical and classical roles. In his poems he runs through the whole gamut of traditional and accepted feelings towards the women he knew closely, they are Madonnas or witches: enchantresses and betrayers, or spiritual guides and embodiments of the Muse: angelic spirits or demonic phantoms. They can play the function of mother, sister, daughter, and equally that of seductress, lover, Siren, corrupter. Rarely, do they take up the position of friend or companion, and it is revealing that Baudelaire failed in his own life to establish such a lasting platonic relationship with a woman, though he came closest perhaps with Madame Sabatier.

He also dramatised internally the presence of the stepfather, General Aupick, a man both initially loved and admired and yet also hated, a man forming with the mother and himself a triangular situation, that Baudelaire found echoed in literature. Baudelaire too is always a spirit in whom contradiction flourishes, in whom the opposites co-exist. Extreme emotion in him can manifest at either end of its spectrum. The reality is that he was born both highly intelligent, and hyper-sensitive, so that he was enthralled by, delighted by, tormented by relationship with women, and also capable of seeing the literary, and imaginative dimensions of those relationships, into which he transported his many frustrations and his desires for the Ideal, for the paradise garden, for Beauty, the intangible mystery, that could remain above life, unshaken by its instability and transience. The image of his mother is present in the *Balcony* [p. 54], that poem D. H. Lawrence quoted and understood so well, where she is lover, queen, sister, though merged with other women. When he sees himself as Hamlet, in *Beatrice* [p. 52], then it is Gertrude, Hamlet's mother, re-marrying the hated stepfather after Hamlet's father's death, who is invoked in the background, a corrupted Beatrice, merging with Ophelia. When he implies the presence of Orestes in mentioning Pylades his friend, and Electra his sister, in the *Voyage* [p. 127], then it is the faithless Clytaemnestra who is conjured, marrying her lover, conniving at the father, Agamemnon's murder, a father avenged by her son.

'La Reine s'Efforce de Consoler Hamlet'
Eugène Delacroix（French, 1798 – 1863）
Yale University Art Gallery

Baudelaire is not totally dominated by memories of his mother: she is superseded by, or incorporated into other women. Woman could be the exotic, strange seductress, personified in Jeanne Duval. She is realised artistically as The *Creole Lady* [p. 14] and The *Woman of Malabar* [p. 15], the tawny mistress of *The Jewels* [p. 44], and the *Snake That Dances* [p. 46], the enchanted garden of *Exotic Perfume* [p. 56] and The *Head of Hair* [p. 57], of *Afternoon Song* [p. 60], who is also the tormentor and betrayer of *Beatrice* [p. 52], and *Je t'adore* [p. 48]. In that role she is primarily a component of Idyll. Despite his stormy relationship with Jeanne Duval, these are poems of literary transformation, mainly of admiration for Woman as animal, as creature, though also ultimately as cruel, and cold enchantress.

Woman too could be a purified sister or child, the *red-headed* [p. 66] beggar girl, or the exotic lover with whom he would sail to her native land in The *Invitation to the Voyage* [p. 82] and its *prose* [p. 85] equivalent, or the lover of The *Death* [p. 63] of Lovers, transubstantiated with him. There is a tenderness within these poems that shows Baudelaire's capacity for affection and respect, that offsets and perhaps belies the compound of disgust, nostalgia and fetishism that his relationship with his mother invoked in him, or the inability to relate sexually and intellectually to Jeanne Duval that shut off from him the often tender poetic world of a Propertius or Ovid, or the interior sacred marriage of a John Donne.

In his relationship with Marie Daubrun, the figure perhaps represented at the end of *The Irreparable* [p. 88] as the theatrical fairy of gold and gauze who 'floored the enormous Satan', she of the green eyes, Woman represents again that tension between the enchantress and the betrayer, between that which might save and that which harms. She is the tender heart of *Autumn Song II* [p. 98], but also the dangerous woman, cold and chilled of that same autumn in *Autumn Sonnet* [p. 100], and is similarly pitiless and wintry in *Clouded Sky* [p. 93] and inimical in The *Poison* [p. 91]. Perhaps *Semper Eadem* [p. 115] reflects again her ability to soothe him by her presence, in a poem that may equally refer to all the women in his life.

With Madame Sabatier, his admiration becomes more intellectual and refined, as if the closer to the Ideal he travelled, the less sexual closeness was a possibility for him. Her presence arouses a deep self-disgust in him that spills over into imaginary sadism in *To She* [p. 101] Who Is Too Light-Hearted, and she (rather than Marie, I think) takes up the position of his

Guardian Angel and his Ideal in *Reversibility* [p. 103], as in *Confession* [p. 105], For Madame *Sabatier* [p. 108], the *Living Torch* [p. 109] (her eyes), and *Hymn* [p. 110] (where she is the immortal idol'). She becomes perhaps an intensified mother-image for him, and so opens the gates of childhood memory in *Moesta* [p. 112] Et Errabunda, and *Harmony* [p. 114] of Evening. It should be understood that for Baudelaire the women in his life merge to become a single, multi-faceted representation of Woman, so that attributing one poem or another to a specific woman fails to convey the complexity of allusion.

Sometimes Baudelaire detached himself from the specific and addressed the intellectual Ideal in pure Romantic fashion. So in *Sorrows* [p. 26] of the Moon, and the *Moon Offended* [p. 165], that cold Ideal of *Beauty* [p. 36] softens and weeps over the lost child, the ruined century. Beauty in anything, specifically beauty in woman opens potential gates for Baudelaire, frees his mind and emotions for voyage into the ocean that soothes the bruised heart and the shattered nerves, but the spectre of sexuality, that which drags the spirit towards the animal, is the force that he can neither deny in himself nor reconcile with his Ideal. Beauty is forced then to reveal itself as a mirror-like emptiness, a gaze of stone or metal, a guarded remoteness to which Baudelaire cannot aspire (In fact eyes appear in many of his poems as the symbols of the mood he is seeking to express, their gaze obscure, or penetrating, fixed or mobile, from the 'familiar looks' of *Correspondences* [p. 43], to the fixed stare of the *Satyresses* [p. 160], from the sweet, tender eyes of *Bertha* [p. 18], to the eyes of *Beauty* [p. 36] 'bright with eternity'.) He must push Beauty away from himself in order to protect it from degradation.

The depth of disgust with himself that this lack of resolution and reconciliation stirs, may derive from the psychical relationship with his mother, and from Catholic teaching, it is true, but it also taps into the ancient enmity between Man the transient force, and Woman the eternal womb, it evokes the dance of the sexes, and illustrates the harmful rather than helpful roles of the woman, her ambiguity as a lover. Madonna, Angel, Muse are positive aspects of Baudelaire's attitude towards her: the roles of sister, and daughter, are more tranquil middle-grounds between two extremes: while the supposedly benign mother, and the tender lover are more difficult roles for him, merging easily with the erotic witch and enchantress, the seducer to excessive love, and the ultimate betrayer. The self-disgust of a great poem *Voyage to Cythera* [p. 74], can seem to sound the key-note of Baudelaire's failure to relate to Woman. In some respects its greatness belies its narrowness and limitation as a work, carrying him back towards conventional religion, portraying him as a sexual failure, or misogynist, a man whose failure in relationship soured his view of existence.

Yet that self-disgust perhaps intensified by his breaking away from Jeanne Duval is not the whole story of Baudelaire, any more than are the difficulties of the relationship with his mother. The sensitivity, the potential for that disgust was born in him, intellect finding disappointment in reality, mind dragged down to body, desire and tenderness thwarted by reticence, and apparent betrayal. We are all, if we are truly aware, sensitised to the difficulty of modern existence. Religion failed Baudelaire in that respect as it fails us: the relationship desired has no analogue in experience: reality opposes the dream. We are left with the apparently absurd, the wasteland, and the fact that the world is not enough for us: or rather that we are too much for the world. Baudelaire's sensitivity and courage made him a precursor who willed himself to confront reality even though he had to seek refuge also in his artificial paradises in order to temporarily escape the pain of being, or at least alleviate it.

Yet again it is not the whole story. The full range of his poetry, from his early idealisations and dream perspectives of the exotic and erotic through his four major relationships including that with his mother, and his nostalgia for that short-lived idyllic period with her, show great tenderness, and an endless yearning for satisfaction through relationship. It is the mistrust of relationship, emphasised by his mother's betrayal perhaps, but essentially an existential condition aligned with modernity, where all relationship has to be self-sustaining, where our relationship with the external universe is in question, that causes his relationships to fail, and presents relationship, or the lack of it in enduring form, as the central issue of Baudelaire's life and art, as it is the central issue of the emotional life of modern humanity. If Woman cannot fill the vacuum the Universe presents Man with, if no Other can fully meet the existential needs of the Self, and the Self is frail, mortal and beleaguered, then Baudelaire's failures are specific examples of a generalised failure of human relationship to populate the Void and grant Humanity the solace it needs. Admittedly that Void is only seen by certain spirits, by certain hyper-sensitive spirits, by certain highly aware, extremely intelligent and rigorously honest spirits, while many seem satisfied with what can be realised in the human condition, but the vision is no less valid for that. Baudelaire cannot be condemned for seeing clearly, and being too stubborn an intellect to accept what he could not find acceptable, or be attacked as too weak a human being merely because he could not cease to long for what he could not realise or achieve.

The Voyage towards Woman did at times fill him with self-disgust. He saw himself as the Hanged Man, the Corpse, as flesh condemned to Hell, divorced forever from Paradise, and praying only for the courage to view himself and his failures clearly. In that mood towards the end of his life in 'My Heart Laid Bare' he sees the need for love as driven merely by a 'horror of solitude, this need to forget the ego in the flesh of another', while the artist 'never emerges from himself'. He describes Woman as having 'nothing except a body', and love-making as 'a crime for which one cannot dispense with an accomplice'. That is a soured and wearied Baudelaire. But his work as a whole does not focus on that traditional and limited extreme view of Woman. The Voyage to Cythera also understands that her island was once the 'Isle of sweet secrets and the heart's delight!' His poetry covers the range, and there is within it the possibility always of tenderness, gentleness, beauty in relationship, of 'those vows, those perfumes, those infinite kisses' of the *Balcony* [p. 54], that might 'be reborn, from gulfs beyond soundings, as the suns that are young again climb in the sky, after they've passed through the deepest of drownings?'

'Le Pendu' – Félicien Rops （Belgian, 1833 – 1898）
LACMA Collections

To view him as, and worse to dismiss him as, impotent, voyeuristic, perverted, a lover of frigid women, contemptuous of the natural, is to believe too readily the words he himself wrote in his journals and elsewhere. One poem like his *Letter* [p. 37] to Saint-Beuve might stress his early intoxication with the idea of the Voluptuary: that does not make Baudelaire one, any more than we become what we read merely because it fascinates us and explains some of our internal thoughts, desires and dreams. Baudelaire used Saint-Beuve's work to understand his own nature, but it does not define him. He always in fact distances his own work from his life. He is a much more self-conscious, self-aware poet than he is often given credit for. In certain moods he can appear exactly what he describes in his prose, he can play those roles, but his sexuality and his view of sexuality was complex, subtle, and contained many shades of awareness and feeling. The readiness with which Baudelaire's work invites analysis, psycho-analysis, speculative destructiveness, negative commentary, should warn us to beware of simplification. His personal life does not exhaust his work, which carries meaning beyond the specific, and it is his work that concerns us here.

Baudelaire in his relationships with women is it is true in many respects an unreconstructed male, a traditionalist, a believer in the polarities. He read widely in the Greek and Roman Classics, and absorbed the Classical idea of the socially unequal though emotionally powerful role of Woman (Ovid was perhaps one of the few Classical writers whose idea of woman was somewhat more enlightened, Euripides another). Baudelaire was also a Christian, and absorbed the same polarised view of Woman often represented by the religion, Madonna or Whore, Mother or Seducer. In that respect he is perhaps not a true modern, but a child of his time, and of the past. But there is validity in understanding Woman's representation for Man in those archetypal and restricted ways, because we are linked by sexual biology and custom to our primitive past, so that Baudelaire's 'love' poems still speak to a modern reader, still realise tensions that remain powerful in our present, in our psyches (male and female) and our society. The sexual can be at war with the intellectual and spiritual in hyper-sensitive and deeply thoughtful minds. Expectation of relationship can still meet with concealment, bewitchment, disappointment, feelings of betrayal. It is the failure of relationship that is at the centre of Baudelaire's poetry: that drives him to the Voyage: that colours and flavours his attitudes, and that proclaims his modernity. His insecurity leads to alienation, his failed paradises reveal the backcloth of hell, and the seething city, with its analogues, the seething oceans of the Siren, the woods filled with the winds' roar, the mire and slime of Nature's corruption, is the landscape where he searches for relationship.

'Jeune Orpheline au Cimetière' - Eugène Delacroix (French, 1798 – 1863)
The Yorck Project: 10.000 Meisterwerke der Malerei, 2002
Directmedia Publishing GmbH - *Wikimedia Commons*

IV: THE CITY (THE VISION OF HELL)

If existence is fallen, if relationship with Deity, or the mother, or the Ideal, has failed, if we are exiled from the external paradise we seek, then it is natural to position ourselves in an analogue of the traditional Hell, whose ruler is the traditional Satan, the Angel who sinned through Pride. The analogue for Dante's City of Dis, where Satan rules, is the modern City, Paris with its crowded streets and arcades, its multiplicity of beings and locations, its many levels and gradations of existence. Satan will be a kind of hero, a mask of the poet, a Prince of Exile as we see in the *Litanies* [p. 32] of Satan. But we are in a strange and somewhat different Hell than that of Dante. The sins of the modern Satanist are not Dante's public sins of violence, evil against others: they are not the sins of heresy, public corruption, or public betrayal of others: they are rather the obsessions and frailties of the modern Self. Those who go looking for the world of a De Sade in Baudelaire are soon disappointed, despite his often colourful mock-Satanic poses. He is essentially a moral man, adrift in modernity's maze, a man of great tenderness ravaged by existential loss. Satan, the poet's image, is the eternally frustrated one, the buried rebel, the dethroned prince of longing. His disciples are the tormented ones, those seeking escape or forgetfulness, solace or oblivion. When they are strong and invigorated, they are proud rebels, seeking, as Baudelaire claims the dandy, the *flâneur*, does in The Painter of Modern Life, to 'combat and destroy the trivial'. They will identify with other rebels, they will as we shall see, become aspects of 'the poet as hero'. When they are weak and damaged they will be the lost tribe of Cain, the wanderers in pain and torment, the driven gamblers of *The Game* [p. 124], and the sad images of ourselves in To The *Reader* [p. 116], the strange tribe of *Seven* [p. 136] Old Men, exiled Wandering Jews, or the sufferers and labourers of the *Evening* [p. 78] and *Morning* [p. 80] Twilight, the damned Lesbian Women, and the inhabitants of the ladder of sins in the *Voyage* [p. 127], in *Calm* [p. 161]. They are our selves: exiles, crooks, whores, gamblers, drinkers, flawed by deadly sins of pride and lust, avarice and envy, by stupidity and meanness, by deceitfulness and cruelty. Dante's Hell is in some sense contained within Baudelaire's, as the public is somehow concealed in the private, but it is the private self, the inner self, the fallen self, that Baudelaire is primarily concerned with.

'La Messagère du Diable' – Félicien Rops (Belgian, 1833 – 1898)
LACMA Collections

And it seems the sinners are not truly evil, as Satan is not demonic. Baudelaire identifies with and sympathises with his victims of existence, those cast into the existential Void, who strive to create means of escape, through infatuation, obsession, opiates, intoxication with wine, beauty, sensuality, those who search for any means of escape, any fruitful relationship, but who end, betrayed, adrift, tormented, imprisoned in the Self, and face to face with spiritual emptiness, with the lassitude of lost ideals and aims, with *Ennui*. This is a realm without Faith, or Hope, and so it can be mapped to Dante's Hell, but equally since there is no Paradise, and no Purgatory except in the sense of a repetition of hell in the internal purgatory of remorse and self-disgust, it can easily be mapped to a modern wasteland, where religion is no longer a meaningful intellectual option, where behaviour and morality must be addressed from the direction of our biological origins, and our imposed 'civilised' values, which if we are to save them must be rooted in creativity opposing destruction, truth opposing falsehood, kindness opposing violence and cruelty, whether physical or spiritual, and empathy forging relationship against the indifference of the intention-less Universe.

The City for Baudelaire is another ocean of isolation, another place where relationship fails. Though he is essentially an apolitical writer, barely non-conformist, his age penetrates his thought and writing, merely because of the potency of the changes happening around him. Paris reveals all the facets of the modern Capitalist citadel. There, Baudelaire explained in an early poem, the prostitute sells her soul to buy shoes, and he too sells his thought, wanting to be an author. The City is a marketplace where the individual is commoditised, and that is a key aspect of Baudelaire's Hell, that the individual, so prominent a feature of Dante's Hell, even among the crowds there, is here submerged in the ant-heap.

'La Musique aux Tuileries' – Édouard Manet (French, 1832 – 1883)
The Yorck Project: 10.000 Meisterwerke der Malerei, 2002
Directmedia Publishing GmbH – *Wikimedia Commons*

In The Painter of Modern Life Baudelaire celebrates the impassioned observer, anonymous spectator at home in the world, entering into the masses, 'a huge reservoir of electrical energy'. The street is a dwelling-place, the crowd is endless interest. Yet already it is the isolated voyeur whom Baudelaire brings before us, the man for whom relationship is with the crowd and not other individuals. It needs a Kierkegaard to penetrate that psychology of the crowd, that mass culture of our age, that statistical murmur of which we are all now part, Kierkegaard, greatest defender of the pass and defile of the Individual. For Baudelaire the masses merely conceal the asocial individual deep in their ranks. He writes of the woman who passes by, the erotic opportunity, that like a flash of lightning arrives and vanishes, fugitive beauty, forever loved and forever unknown. The crowd, its anonymity, offers here the perfect realisation of the Ideal, that which can be seen, which enters into the lonely soul, but like a figure in a painting, a character in a novel, can never be compromised by new and extraneous knowledge. She is a Beatrice who cannot be corrupted by reality: Beatrice mourned and loved from afar.

For the individual who fails in relationship the City is a haven, full of interest, human interest, but divorced from self, complex, requiring no engagement, yet inviting it, while seducing us. In the City individuals as Sartre noted, fulfil roles, submerge themselves. So the gambler, the drinker, the seeker of anonymous sex, the thief, the beggar, the whore, the dandy, the voyeur, can move in secret, though wholly visible, so long as they play their parts well. It is theatre. It is Vanity Fair. Yet human beings become numbers, their output becomes a commodity: their identity becomes the trail of their public transactions, nature is distanced. The sensitive person who longs for intimate relationship is both enthralled and appalled by the seething of the crowd, seduced by its anonymity and sense of protection, its glitter and enchantment, its confusion of classes and tasks, contrasted with its distinctions of levels and gradations, yet also annihilated by its emptiness and indifference, its ruthless commoditisation and its existence beyond the transient components that happen at any time to comprise it. At night it is a strange new ocean, populated by denizens of the deep and surface shoals, glittering with lights like the hidden universe, concealing and revealing.

'Masques Parisiens' – Félicien Rops （Belgian, 1833 – 1898）
LACMA Collections

In The Painter of Modern Life, Baudelaire was experiencing the first stage of this urbanisation effect. His Paris still has a high degree of intimacy and individuality, yet by reason of its complexity and size it can act as a potent drug on the dulled mind, both stimulating and refreshing. Later as his Paris changes, as he finds it harder to manage the shadows and the miseries, it becomes an ocean on which the exile floats, a night through which he wanders, a dark wood in which he is storm-bound, its resting-places are barren rocks, its inhabitants are downed birds, lost sailors, abandoned spirits. The human wreckage: the human disaster, the submergence of the individual, the repetition of beings within roles, all become more apparent as Baudelaire's perspective darkens. He himself detests progress and industry (but not individual work, that to him was sacred) and yet realises that the landscape of his own city verses owes much to the changes modernity is bringing about. He has deep empathies but they are not translated into humanitarian action, which is another aspect of Baudelaire's apolitical nature, his concern with self and its sensitivities, his lack of relationship. He looks into Hell, he wanders its streets, among the fiery tombs, and the icy lakes, the pools of slime, and the rocky deserts, just as Dante does, but though his keynote is also pity, and though he does not condemn so much as identify with Hell's denizens, his journey through it leads to no program of change, no discipline that progresses us towards Paradise. Paradise is achieved if at all by escape, for here there is no God, and no hope of salvation, only of miraculous transformation within, through fantasy, delirium, art, dream, or voyage. This Hell is Hell, as in Dante, eternal, a state of loss, of stasis, of fracture, of separation, where relationship is doomed, but compared with Dante's Hell it is one with no way out, other than the journey within.

Baudelaire's work, unlike Hugo's or Dickens', is not filled with descriptions of the City. His Paris appears, as in The Swan [p. 143], as almost a Classical backcloth, otherwise it is conjured by subtle hints, by mood and feel, as in The Seven Old Men [p. 136], or in Epilogue [p. 157]. The crowd is present, even in the deserted dawn, as a spectral throng, Dante's masses on the shore of Acheron, present as the hosts of the dead in the anatomical plates of the bookseller's stalls, present in the repetition of old men, the wandering Jew multiplied by identity, or the shrivelled old women. Baudelaire supports the Individual, separated from this Hellish mob, yet in his weaker moments he identified with the mob. In Baudelaire the city implies the crowd, the crowd implies the city. The place where relationship fails is also the series of faces with whom it fails, the sets of eyes that gaze at the single one, sad *pensive* [p. 15] eyes, *fixed* [p. 143] eyes, the eyes of the lost beings who in that powerful poem *Obsession* [p. 152] leap from his eyes onto the canvas of shadows, uniting the crowds defeated by Nature with those defeated and exiled by society. Incidentally, as previously suggested, a whole book could be written on the eyes that appear in Baudelaire's poems, of every colour from green to blood red, carrying every mood from languor to venom, from seductiveness to fixity, eyes of interrogation, repose, trance, witchcraft, darkness, the windows of the spirit, and its pools of oblivion also.

For Baudelaire the City is the Crowd, and it is also the Ocean, the Forest trees, the shadows of Night, all of those giant arenas which correspond to it, and which also transmute the crowd into the lost ranks of the dead, the drowned voyagers, the familiar shades from which the Self is severed. Among the crowd the lonely man can make contact with the anonymous Ideal, or be terrified by the monotony of repetition, can single out the mirror of the Self, or be lost in the multiple echoing images of the multitude.

It is interesting to trace this altering City in his poetry as it develops through time. In the early poems, for example in *Landscape* [p. 22], the City is an enchanted world, above which a further enchanted world lies, inhabited by the poet separated from the Crowd, its workshops full of 'song and light'. The belfries and towers are masts of voyaging ships, or vessels in a vast harbour, and the solitary poet can conjure an Idyll in imagination that transcends the City but is launched from its eyries. Similarly in *The Sun* [p. 24], the City is a place of possibilities where the lone poet can wander receiving inspiration, while the same poetic sun that warms his spirit enters and warms the City. In both poems the Crowd is absent, temporarily stilled, barred from access, abandoned below, or rendered invisible.

By the time of *Evening* [p. 78] and *Morning* [p. 80] Twilight, the City is a populated ant-heap with recognisable characters that arouse empathy. These are exiles too, lost on the ocean of shadows, at dawn or evening. The *Irreparable* [p. 88] without mentioning the City specifically shows nevertheless an illuminated screen where the shadows of the defeated Crowd pass, where only in the theatre does the fantasy of Hope stir. Further on, in

Moesta [p. 112] Et Errabunda it has become a sordid city, a city of slime and remorse. As Baudelaire lives beyond his close relationships with women, and becomes more isolated, so the darkened image of the City and the Crowd of the damned intensifies. With To The *Reader* [p. 116], and *The Game* [p. 124], we are among the crowd of obsessed, sinful spirits, images of ourselves, of the average human being, locked in place in the stasis of Hell. The *Seven* [p. 136] Old Men shows us a terrifying vision of monstrous repetition and multiplication, of exile and spiritual desolation, where the only image Baudelaire can find for his own soul is (as in Rimbaud's 'The Drunken Boat') a 'mastless barge' on a 'monstrous sea', perfect symbol of the defeated vessel of the Individual, adrift on the storm-tossed ocean of the City.

Finally in the *Draft Epilogue* [p. 155] and *Epilogue* [p. 157], and in *Calm* [p. 161], the City is once more a backcloth only now a backcloth for the exhausted spirit, for the weary alchemist who has 'turned mud into gold', whose heart is quiet, who at last finds calm. It is a tribute to Baudelaire's monumental construction of his poetic work, his slow, tenacious building of an almost Classical oeuvre, that we can see these steady changes in his perception of the City and the Crowd as his life changes, and he becomes increasingly sensitive to failed relationship, lost ideals, and the ambivalence of the City that provided him with an ever-changing background, a strange intense landscape, but also challenged his very being with its ultimate indifference to him, an indifference in which at the last he finds refuge.

And Satan is absent, or all-but absent. The City of Dis is not the City of a heroic Satan, but a place of alienation, something Baudelaire also learnt from Dante, whose Satan, when we reach him at the base of the Inferno, is a ludicrous monster from whom emanates an absurd gale of darkness, that has no need to stir and fuel Hell, because it is in a sense impotent to alter the stasis of the infernal regions with their eternally repetitive punishments, and their masses of shades without hope, progression, or even, in the depths, language. And this City is not the city of the Revolution, the failed revolution spiritually, in that it brought nothing to the masses but a new kind of slavery. It is the City of Modernity, of the future, where Revolution is defused by wealth and urbanisation, by mechanisation and acceptance. Baudelaire is no revolutionary, he is a witness.

'La Foire aux Amores' – Félicien Rops (Belgian, 1833 – 1898)
LACMA Collections

Here, in this City of Dis, the sins are not sins against Deity but sins against Self: against Mind and Imagination. Crime is significant rather than sin, and crime, as theft, prostitution, avarice, stupidity, is spiritual laziness, an obsession to match the other obsessions of the spirit, pride, lust, longing, remorse, regret, memory even: it is an opiate to dull the senses. The City itself is a commoditised space, a theatre for the Crowd, with which the true Individual cannot identify. Here there is no Catullus, or Horace. Paris is not Classical Rome, and the poet is in exile from the social nexus, wherever that may be located. How completely Baudelaire in his poetry cuts himself off from the society of his time, from his own class, his peers! Whatever his situation in life, his situation in the poetry is carefully determined and subtly penned. He identifies with the outcasts, the pariahs, the obsessed, the defeated, and not with the successful, the wealthy, the powerful, and yet he is never a rebel as such, and in the end is like Dante 'a party of one', a spiritual onlooker, for whom the City is symbol but never an entity with which he has a true relation, any more than he has with Nature.

Baudelaire is ultimately not a poet of the City or the Crowd, as say Hugo was, or Dickens. He is not in profound relation. He identifies and draws back, he empathises and scorns. He is no lover of the people, no democrat, no Walt Whitman. Baudelaire is too full of disgust with the human condition, too full of self-disgust to champion a humanity he has lost faith in. His city dwellers are not the respectable citizens, who hardly appear, they are those whose lives depend on transience, on chance, on the repetition of the valueless instant, they are opportunistic thieves, gamblers whose fate depends on the next moment, on randomness: they are prostitutes seeking the next encounter, the repetition of previous encounters: they are beggars and rag-pickers searching the mire. They are not creative workers, builders, artists, but the flotsam and jetsam of the mindless ocean, the recipients of the fruits of anonymity, those who have fallen out of relationship, and whose public lives do not require relationship except with the ephemeral. The prostitute is the archetypal symbol of this commercialised, commoditised society, one who is the physical commodity and the seller, the shop-window and the store, the product and the service combined. Relationship with a prostitute, such as Jeanne Duval almost certainly was, exists in that overlap between the fixed social world of work and home, and the fluid world of the ephemeral City. Baudelaire was attracted by that overlap, that twilight, that boundary between raw and cooked, wild and tame, land and sea. 'Why,' he asked, 'does the man of intellect prefer whores to society women, although both types are equally stupid? Find the answer?' The answer is in the freedom that such a meeting offers: freedom from oppressive, fixed, or failed relationships, freedom for new relationship. *Ennui* drives Baudelaire towards such a meeting, disappointment and disgust finally drive him away. Jeanne Duval was not a path to the ideal or the Idyll: and unfortunately Marie Daubrun and Madame Sabatier were not paths to satisfaction and solace either. The City is always for Baudelaire a source of interest, a source of mystery, an ocean for anonymous voyage, a place of concealed freedoms, and yet it also leads through observation of its denizens, and entry into its whirlpool, to sadness, shame and alienation.

The City, the Crowd, is where pride may be exhibited, fame may be won, relationship may be established, the Mind may be stimulated, life may be enjoyed, and yet, for the shy man, the anxious man, the hyper-sensitive man, the man for whom relationship with the Other is difficult, who finds it hard to emerge from himself, it is also where humiliation may be exacted, failure may become evident, the Mind may be dulled by obsession and disappointment, life may be constrained and dissipated. It is one more Ocean of the Voyage.

V: VOYAGE TO MODERNITY (THE VISION OF LIMITATION)

B audelaire's Voyage was a voyage in search of relationship. Voyage is movement, it expresses possibility, opens horizons, re-energises hope. The ship, the vessel, a persistent symbol for him, is like us a wanderer, happier than us through its insentience, beautiful in its form (at least the fully-rigged sailing ship that Baudelaire knew was), a wanderer of far distances, a traveller to exotic countries, always arriving, resting, setting out again, rocked by the waves as in a cradle. 'A harbour is a charming retreat for a soul weary of life's struggles' says Baudelaire in his prose poems (XLI The Harbour) going on to describe the slender vessels in their harmonious oscillations. The *Invitation* [p. 82] to the Voyage and its *prose* [p. 85] equivalent celebrate them: 'nomads' who 'come from the ends of the world', 'huge ships charged with riches' which are his own 'enriched thoughts'. The vessels are quasi-living entities, beings like us who search for eternity, for the Idyll, for the Ideal, only more blessed than us, cradled by the ocean, carrying memories of childhood in their rocking motion, sensations of intimacy, symmetry and beauty. They evoke 'the notion of a huge creature, complicated but rhythmical, an animal full of genius, suffering and sighing with all the ambitions of mankind.' (Rockets XXII). 'These great, handsome ships, swaying imperceptibly, cradled so to speak, on the tranquil waves: these strong ships, with their aura of idleness and nostalgia, surely they ask us, silently: 'When do we set sail for happiness?'' (Rockets XI). Ships have identities: they are those almost-living hulls of Virgil's that populate the Aeneid (See especially Cybele's transformation of the Trojan fleet in Book IX). They are the steeds of heroes: of Odysseus, or the Argonauts.

'Embarquement de Folkestone' – Édouard Manet (French, 1832 – 1883)
The Yorck Project: 10.000 Meisterwerke der Malerei, 2002
Directmedia Publishing GmbH – *Wikimedia Commons*

The ship at anchor is the poet waiting for inspiration, indolent in the creative sense, yet rigged out, ready for travel, waiting a favourable breeze. It is strong, sturdy, solid, a potential hero. Far horizons beckon to it, its path is not yet charted: its destinations are not yet visible: the unknown entices, the undiscovered calls. When it sets sail it becomes the image of all wanderers, all Classical travellers, all escapees from our many internal and external prisons, and so analogous with every nomad, gypsy, every great bird in flight, and the ocean on which it sails is a symbol of every other ocean into which we plunge, where we swim, whose waves we traverse, the oceans of Woman and sensuality, of the City, of intoxication, obsession and dream, of night and twilight, of the Other whose eyes absorb us, of Nature's great forests, sunsets and seasons, of Time, Space, Mind, action, desire.

And if Baudelaire were only the poet of these things, of tranquil harbours, of setting sail, of calm voyages and ecstasy in the depths, then he would remain the Romantic poet, *le romantique transcendant* that Flaubert claimed him to be, a classic of that genre. But Baudelaire is only rarely the poet of these things. He does indeed touch on the beauties and the enchantments, none more brilliantly, so that the images from his poems of ships at rest, or setting out on their voyage stay with us, fiercely and sweetly delineated. But Baudelaire's true voyage is towards Modernity, and so his voyages end not in enchanted isles, rather they are voyages to *Cythera* [p. 74], or to the distant but disappointing destinations of his greatest poem The *Voyage* [p. 127], from which bored travellers return to report scathingly the tedious news of the whole world. His exotic women end as debased exiles, the *Woman of Malabar* [p. 15], or Andromache that tragic heroine passed through many hands, and the lost consumptive negress of *The Swan* [p. 143]. His wanderers, his *gypsies* [p. 69], travel towards the realm of shadows, 'eyes grown heavier, with mournful regret for absent visions'. His city dwellers are doomed to the transience, resignation, decrepitude, and repetition of their doomed landscape. The great birds fall from the sky, symbols, as is *Icarus* [p. 166] of the aspiring artist, of the poet himself, crippled like the *Albatross* [p. 17] on earth, damaged and dying like the *Swan* [p. 143]. The wiser *Owls* [p. 65] recommend caution. Nature too creates fear rather than beauty as in *Obsession* [p. 152], or emphasises the sadness of transience as in *Autumn Song* [p. 98], or the pain of existence as in *Music* [p. 72]. And even in death, which seems perhaps a gateway at the end of The *Voyage* [p. 127] or in *Death* [p. 71] of the Poor, even there it seems the dream is corrupted, the *carcase* [p. 49] of beauty rots, the *skeletons* [p. 139] of the dead dig forever in an enigmatic landscape.

Baudelaire begins his voyage seeking, as he says of Guys in his essay on him, 'the transitory, fleeting beauty of our present existence, the characteristics of what the reader has allowed us to call *modernism.*' But Baudelaire is not the poet of that beauty alone, it co-exists in his work with clarity of thought, a depth of feeling that is in tension with that beauty. Modernity is the realisation of limitation. Romanticism in its failure to find an objective state corresponding to its desires for the Ideal, and the Idyll, ends in *Ennui*, in a spiritual impasse. It is Baudelaire's greatness as a poet to transmute that mud into gold, to extract poetic riches from unpromising material, to blend the dream and the enchantment with the harsh reality, so that we are presented with the latter veiled by the former. Poetic form and beauty of language and imagery allow us closer to the reality while still protected to some degree from its full impact.

On occasions Baudelaire's poetry can create an illusion of modernity where it is in fact highly traditional. Poems like *Beatrice* [p. 52], which reveals the faithless mistress or *A Rotting Carcase* [p. 49] composed on the theme of the mistress's and beauty's mortality, connect to a formal poetic past, here Classical and Medieval respectively (there is a Renaissance connection also for example with the poetry of Ronsard), but Baudelaire infuses even these poems with a sense of the deep yearning for the Ideal, the Idyll, Paradise, a longing, compromised by reality, that takes us well beyond those previous periods, while retaining a classical and medieval solidity and sense of the real, that likewise takes us beyond Romanticism. No Roman writer, no Ovid, Horace or Virgil desires to escape from reality as much as this, or is so inimical to daily life, so desperate to go beyond the given. Classicism ultimately enjoys its world, and even enjoys the formal speculation about the after-life. There is an irony in Latin Classicism towards its subject matter, a half-veiled disbelief in the deities that populate its world, a sophisticated transformation of the Greek inheritance, and Baudelaire relates to that, and inherits that irony, transferring it to the Christian ethos. But it is the intensity of Christian belief, now denied that fuels Baudelaire's intensity, an intensity that is not found in the gentle laughter and calm speculation of the less intense Romans. No Medieval writer has so little faith in the other aspects of the afterlife that offset the terror and disgust of mortality and deceit. Baudelaire is in Hell with no Paradise: while the Classical world doubted Hell and Paradise: the Medieval world believed in both: and the Renaissance world was prepared to give the benefit of the doubt to faith.

'Le Vice Suprême' – Félicien Rops (Belgian, 1833 – 1898)
LACMA Collections

Some of Baudelaire's inferior poetry is too full of the pose (or reality) of the tormented poet to engage us closely now, it smacks of the hysteria of Romanticism rather than its clarity. Many of his poems, The *Balcony* [p. 54] is a very fine example, are expressions of desire and longing, of escape and reverie, modern in tone because they take internal rather than external routes: society, religion, metaphysics etc offering no obvious paths to the poet. But perhaps his greatest poems bring us face to face with reality, in terms which do engage, and do stay with us as defining images of the human predicament in the modern world. It is useful to pick out some of these great keynote poems that punctuate the voyage.

The *Albatross* [p. 17], is the first such poem: it brings Romanticism to earth, or rather to the deck, and the Poet is presented as a creature blessed with spiritual and intellectual wings but grounded by reality, and doomed to constraint and limitation. *Beatrice* [p. 52] is a self-revealing, defining though still traditional moment, where Woman is seen as the betrayer and the poet as a shadow of Hamlet, a player of roles, a distressed modern tormented by the mocking face of the real. The two poems taken together define the poet as a limited, distressed creature, who will be failed by his deepest attempts at relationship, that with the empowering voyage of the spirit through Nature and the universe, and that with Woman, the beloved Other, who as mother, lover, and companion will betray or abandon the loving heart to a desolate relation-less state.

If the Ideal and the Idyll are illusions, if lust torments the body and corrupts and condemns the spirit, if reality tears apart the enchanted isles of relationship, then the poet is the Hanged Man of 'Voyage To *Cythera* [p. 74]'. This magnificent poem, though again its attitudes can be seen as somewhat closed and traditional, presents clearly the failure of Romantic Love, and relationship, when face to face with the self-disgust that the body imposes on the spirit. Utilising the symbolism of voyaging it anticipates, in its imagery and tone, his greatest poem, *The Voyage* [p. 127], while remaining focused on this one dimension of the search for the Ideal, and its resulting failure. The second, greater poem develops out of this first less ambitious concept.

Moesta Et Errabunda [p. 112] reveals the next major attempt to reclaim paradise, and the next confrontation with and realisation of reality. Madame Sabatier is probably addressed here, and their shared frustration is a call to another desperate voyage, towards a virgin sea that might console the poet, through an escape from the city and from suffering, and a regaining (with Madame Sabatier as the mother figure) of childhood innocence with its pre-sexual longings. It is an attempt to go beyond Woman, or rather to return to the cradle, the womb, the harbour where everything is still possible. But its closing lines already anticipate the failure of the journey backwards, there is no return.

To The Reader [p. 116], like a lesser poem *The Game* [p. 124], offers a condemnation of modern humanity, its meanness and triviality rather than its great sinfulness: these damned souls even 'lack fire'! The poem is a symphony of a city it hardly mentions, and while it may seem caustic in its litany of failure, it is also empathetic in its conclusion. This world is the world of the reader, but also the poet. Baudelaire condemns himself along with us all. We are the voyeurs of reality, filled with *Ennui*, not merely boredom, but spiritual barrenness, dreaming of action and sin while solacing ourselves with meaningless pleasures. *The Game* [p. 124], *Spleen* [p. 126], and *Obsession* [p. 152] form a fine lesser trio, emphasising this strange Hell of the lost and defeated, the limited and confined, driven by their repetitious obsessions, filled with tedium or fear, longing for escape, devoid of faith in the spirit or the afterlife, and willing to accept even the torments of their modern Hell to the nothingness of the abyss, to death and annihilation.

Ideas and imagery from all these poems contributed to Baudelaire's central masterpiece, *The Voyage* [p. 127]. Here, in Part I, childhood has embraced the illusion of a vast universe, of life as a great adventure, but now memory realises the pettiness of existence and the smallness of the world. With his opening verse Baudelaire severs himself from any return to childhood innocence, and already anticipates for us the results of the voyage. The ocean, every ocean, is a sea where we take our desires, longing to be soothed, and longing to escape from all our failed attempts at capturing the Ideal, through ambition and work, through a return to childhood, or through that seductive Circe, Woman. The escaping traveller stuns himself with experience to mute the pain and destroy the longing, while the truest travellers voyage out of pure restlessness, a Faustian discontent that demands their endless flight towards the phantasms of their dreams.

'À un Diner d'Athées' – Félicien Rops (Belgian, 1833 – 1898)

LACMA Collections

Part II shows us, as in a mirror, our mad pursuit, spurred on by our malaise and by curiosity, of Love, Fame or Happiness, only to find the barren reef, the deserted rocky isle, the mirages of Eldorado, Capua, the New World. Parts III and IV bring us the traveller's tale, the report from our peers around the globe, the news from everywhere. Cities and landscapes fail to reveal the promise we dreamed, Man and Nature cannot satisfy us. Pleasure only fuels fresh desire, without satisfying our lust for the Ideal and the Idyll. The travellers bring back the exotic for our delectation, the curiosities of strange religions, foreign women, descriptions of architecture, knowledge of all the sights. None of that attracts for long. What else has the traveller found?

Parts V and VI bring us the dreadful truth. Everywhere is here. All is the same. *Ennui* is indeed this vision of the world as repetition. Travelling to foreign countries is no longer travelling towards difference and even perhaps enlightenment, it is travelling towards sameness, towards the human selves we cannot leave behind, but are obliged always to take with us, towards the ladder of sin and corruption that is ours also, towards the failed relationship of the sexes, towards the corruptions of violence and power, the evasions, hypocrisies and illusions of religion, towards the same narcotics and obsessions, the same drugs and vanities, that we find at home. How brilliantly Baudelaire paints the appalling picture: he almost sculpts the condemnation of our human world out of some bright yet veined classical stone. How clearly he anticipates the endless *Ennui* of the modern world, of unsatisfactory restless tourism, of media chatter, of petty dictators and small wars, of relentless hypocrisy and blindness, of damaging triviality and blandness, a world that has to lull itself with drugs and pleasures, with entertainments, with those last voyages that are in reality only voyages around the bay.

Part VII cements the vision in place. It is ourselves, our own Self that we will find, 'our image beckoning' to us in 'a desert of *ennui*.' Time is the enemy, tormenting us, yet still even now sometimes spurring us on, until we hear once more the Siren voices, calling us towards the shores of the Lotus Eaters, like noble, long-suffering Odysseus and his men, or tempting us, like Orestes, the exile and destined avenger of those betrayers, his mother and stepfather, towards relationship: Friendship personified by Orestes' friend Pylades, or Love of family, of innocence, in the form of his sister Electra.

So to Part VIII: if we have done the rounds of our world, if it can offer nothing more than tedium, weariness, boredom, if all our attempts at reaching the Ideal fail, if the Idyll cannot satisfy, if all is doomed to repetition, if we are to be like *Sisyphus* [p. 70] rolling his rock forever up the slope only to watch it roll down, like Tantalus stretching for food he can never reach, like Ixion bound eternally on a wheel of sameness, or like Prometheus condemned to be tormented, torn by the birds, and then restored for fresh torment: if that is our fate, then Death may be preferable, Death alone may offer a voyage beyond this sterility, into whatever realm lies beyond, Hell or Heaven, who cares, but at least something new.

The Voyage [p. 127] is Baudelaire's clearest, most 'classical', and most accomplished attempt to encapsulate the ills of himself and his age, to explain the apparent failure of our relationships with the world, with Nature, with ourselves, and with each other, and in so doing he literally brings on Modernity, and thereby instigates all our attempts since to redefine the human condition in terms that confirm, evade or deny his conclusions. I will discuss those attempts briefly later.

Baudelaire was left at the end of his life to recapitulate the themes of his previous poetry, in terms primarily of loss and sadness, disappointment and at least partial failure (of his personal life though not of his art). Among these, two great poems of Modernity stand out. Firstly The *Swan* [p. 143], a poem which returns in sadness to a Paris that is changing, a Paris of the widowed, the exiled like Ovid, the fallen like the shattered swan itself, biting the dust, the lost like the consumptive negress searching for her idyllic and exotic homeland, the orphaned, the shipwrecked, the imprisoned, the defeated. The mood is one of deep melancholy. The scene is one of transience and decay. These are Classical ruins, pointed by the references to the unhappy Andromache, wife of the broken warrior, Hector, widow of all dead heroes, and by the wolf-mother Sorrow, who akin to the mythical wolf that suckled Romulus and Remus Rome's founders, nourishes the modern age. Andromache is *our* symbol, she who has suffered at the hands of Achilles, and his son, and whose 'false Simois', and smaller version of Troy in exile, are like our diminished age and art compared with the greater ages that are behind us, from which we are exiled, defeated by the conquerors, Time and Fate.

'Le Werwolf' – Félicien Rops（Belgian, 1833 – 1898）
LACMA Collections

The other poem that emerges from this late cluster, perfect though chilling, is *The Void* [p. 164]. The Voyage led to the abyss, and now Baudelaire will describe it, echoing Pascal's Void, the immense spaces that terrified him, an abyss like that which Goethe's Mephistopheles offers us, where all is valueless because all is doomed to extinction, where Time defeats all our actions, dreams, desires, and even our words, even the Word of revelation. Whatever 'God' he speaks of here seems not to be on our side. Is this religion he mentions? Is Baudelaire religious? Or is 'God' merely his name for the forces of fate and time that toy with him? The torment is of being denied nothingness, being condemned to being and number, names and forms as Buddhism would say perhaps, the illusions that entrap us, and prevent us from achieving Nirvana, acceptance, resolution, ultimate relationship with the Universe. If Baudelaire's 'God' exists, he is being distanced from humanity, and is hardly a god of Love.

So the Voyage ends in the abyss, or at least in the fear of it, the fear of its being no more a resolution of our spiritual and emotional suffering and torment than reality is.

Baudelaire has further poems to write after The Void. He even appears to drift towards a religious conclusion in The Unforeseen, but we should remember the ironic note Baudelaire attached to that poem: 'Here the author of Les Fleurs du mal is turning towards the eternal life. It had to end that way. Let us observe that like all the newly-converted, he is very strict and very fanatical.' He learnt his irony towards religion perhaps from Ovid, from that late pagan world that believed and doubted simultaneously.

VI: THE POET AS HERO (THE VISION OF ICARUS)

Where does the immensity of that Voyage, the bleakness of that Vision, leave the poet as a human being? To answer that we must consider Baudelaire's view of poetry and of himself as a poet, his view of the role the poet might adopt in modernity. 'No one listens to the wind which will blow on us tomorrow, yet the heroism of modern life surrounds us and presses in on us' he said. 'The artist, the true artist, will be the one who can extract what is epic from modern life.' Understanding the nature of his age, the terrible forces that are ranged against the individual, the 'cheapening of hearts', the 'coarsening of our natures' (Rockets XXII), that industrialisation and commercialisation inflict, the degree to which the life and the courage of the spirit are weakened by an obstacle beyond our strength, the formless nature of our times, understanding all that, Baudelaire nevertheless demanded the poet adopt the role of hero. It takes a heroic mind to live modernity. To give shape to it is the labour of a Hercules. Nowadays we cannot set out to describe 'the' world (even Baudelaire still had that asset to a degree, the beauties and charms of his 'period') we must first create 'a' world, a consistent image of the world, our own internal version of it, before we can write it: just as we must create a consistent range of words and phrases to encapsulate it. The artist, the poet, is a maker of worlds not a describer of them. Yes, that was always true. Art is art, a creation. But modernity requires a greater trial of strength, a repeated task of clearing away the jostling of the crowd, the multiplicity of signs and signals: a repeated assault like *Sisyphus* [p. 70] on his rock. And the heroism is without hope, *Ennui* is at the door, and no easy answers will suffice. What is required is a massive act of will, across a lifetime, to create an art whose surface value may appear barely commensurate with the effort (where after all is our Divine Comedy, our Metamorphoses, our Odyssey?). Yet as Baudelaire asks himself, is the achievement not perhaps 'infinitely more worthy, because it triumphed in a hostile atmosphere and place'.

Take a hypersensitive man, and set him down in a seething modern city, let him understand the problems of relationship, personal, social, spiritual, in such a place. Is not the ordinary man, a hero, the ordinary woman a heroine to carve a life out of such a chaos? And the poor, the wretched, the derelict, the non-conformist, those living the most ephemeral of lives, represent for Baudelaire the wreckage of the city's tempest. He does not identify with them, except symbolically. He is not a revolutionary, an activist, a rebel, or a saint. He stands apart even as he describes and empathises. He is a witness: I refuse to say a voyeur.

In the beginning Baudelaire is a Romantic, it is Romanticism that first projects the poet as hero: that begins to be self-aware, to construct its own myth, in a mode derived from Dante, himself the protagonist of that great journey through the three realms. In *Landscape* [p. 22], and *The Sun* [p. 24], we see the young poet positioning himself above or outside the crowd in a seemingly empty city, or one where the poet is strangely separated from others, already exercising an act of will, creating self-sufficiently from his own being, identifying with the solitary and remote sun that brings light to the masses, a duellist in Dumas mode fighting for his art. In *Sorrows* [p. 26] of the Moon, and *Beauty* [p. 36], we see that poets are a race apart, that the solitary poet identifies with the distant, narcissistic and languid Moon, that poets are the docile lovers of remote beauty inspired to create, as slaves to the Ideal. These are romantic ideas, not particularly original with Baudelaire, but beautifully expressed by him, and showing already his unique approach.

With *Don Juan* [p. 27] in Hell, we have a picture of the isolated 'hero', the individualist, gazing quietly at the sea of reality, and illusion, proud and scornful, choosing and accepting his own destiny even crossing the Acheron. The image will return at the end of *The Voyage* [p. 127] as the poet asks Captain Death to weigh anchor and float us into the unknown, into the new.

On *Tasso* [p. 29] In Prison, gives us the poet as distraught genius, stifled and imprisoned by the world, in a scene with romantic and baroque overtones, while *Elevation* [p. 41] is a pure declaration of the prize to be won by willed isolation, by mental activity, by the search for the higher and purer. As often with Baudelaire he uses an image of flight to stress freedom, individuality, and the powers of self-willed ascent that winged things symbolise. When defeat and failure comes it will be symbolised by fall, like the fall of proud Satan, into the pit of reality.

'Les Gitanos' – Édouard Manet (French, 1832 – 1883)
Yale University Art Gallery

As Baudelaire's art develops, as life becomes more difficult, as the Ideal comes to seem unattainable, he deepens his position. The poet is doomed to disappointment and perhaps ultimate defeat and failure, in a world inimical to him and to the Ideal. He is to be identified with other beings who strive against the odds, especially those who are exiled or underprivileged but still proud, like the *Red-Headed* [p. 66] Beggar Girl, or the Wandering *Gypsies* [p. 69], doomed to frustration like *Sisyphus* [p. 70], or the *Lesbian* [p. 30] Women, those Greek-style Sapphic victims of a wrong-headed society, 'modern woman in her heroic manifestation'. He creates and celebrates, in the face of mortality, as in A *Rotting Carcase* [p. 49], denying, in Renaissance fashion, the claims of Death to ultimate sovereignty. In *Je t'adore* [p. 48], he attempts to assault, heroically, an implacable and unattainable objective, like some Giant of old attacking Olympus.

Satan [p. 32] is his patron in all this, Satan a symbol of undefeated pride, the guardian of arcane wisdom, the teacher of alchemical skills of transmutation, the champion of the resolute and defiant, spirit of hope and consolation among the exiled and the damned. This is the true sense in which Baudelaire is a Satanist, that Satan is a divinity for him of the oppressed, not an inspirer of crude or violent acts of body or mind. So Satan cannot be relinquished as an idea, and the blasphemy of some of Baudelaire's worst verse is in the end a protest against a God and a religion to which he cannot give ultimate consent, for the sake of those lost in the Inferno, because they are human, with human weaknesses. It is the position of the intellectual rebel, but it leads not to action in Baudelaire, only to the creation of a testament, the testament of modernity.

The hero of the modern world traverses modernity, and is attacked and savaged by it. For him the social contract is broken, since the laws and the virtues condemn so many to exile and failure, disappointment and defeat, yet Baudelaire distances himself from both the worker and the bourgeois, from both the criminal and the justice system. He always moves back, and moves away. He should never be recruited by his commentators into the ranks of the revolutionaries. Baudelaire is an heir of the failed revolutions of the spirit, and of the successful revolutions of matter, commerce, industry. He prophesies the permanence of exile, the completion of mechanisation, the eternal separation of the poet as hero from his Ideal. He both loves and hates his world, as one loves and hates the hell of one's obsessions, the charms of one's lost struggles: the flavour of one's failures. Human existence is surrounded by, hedged about by, filled with, contradiction, irony, paradox, ambiguity, and against these things which defy logic, annihilate our efforts, and entangle us in irresolvable mysteries we have only our willpower, our concentrated labour aimed towards form, understanding, resolution, consolation. We must walk the City of Hell, like the poet himself, in The *Seven* [p. 136] Old Men, steeling our nerves 'like a hero', to face the strangeness of modernity.

Yet the modern mind does not create heroes, it acts them, and so the end is pre-ordained, since the drama is already complete. Baudelaire is a shadow of Hamlet, an actor on holiday, and the *Beatrice* [p. 52] to his Dante is to his mind as faithless as the Ophelia of his imaginings. In The *Voyage* [p. 127] he is Orestes returning from exile to create a bloody denouement, summoned by a phantom Pylades, by a phantom Electra. Despite his claims to heroism, Baudelaire does not dwell on heroes. His Classical allusions are infrequent, though telling, and he does not play intellectually with heroic concepts, rather he makes a passing reference to figures carved in the stone of past art. His real-life poetic heroes were exiled or imprisoned, *Ovid* [p. 153], Dante, *Tasso* [p. 29]. His mind moved rapidly beyond the heroic, to the anti-heroic, the failed attempt, the stricken character, the banished and destroyed.

So he reserves his most potent symbolism for some of his greatest poems. The *Albatross* [p. 17] and The *Swan* [p. 143] are symbols of doom, downed heroes, great birds made for freedom, for winged flight through the heavens, coursing over the waters, embodiments of beauty when at liberty, symbols of defeat and limitation when out of their own habitat, fated to be grounded and handled by human beings. Women too, symbols of beauty, become images of defeat, women traduced, objectified, like his negresses defiled in the city streets, searching for their lost paradises, like Andromache, wife and widow of a hero, become the cast-off prize from a fallen city, Troy, and diminished by exile. Like *Agathe* [p. 112] (Madame Sabatier, Marie?) a victim of her beauty, her sadness, who is imprisoned by the city, by the ocean, by the crowd.

'Hamlet et Horatio au Cimetière' – Eugène Delacroix (French, 1798 – 1863)
The Yorck Project: 10.000 Meisterwerke der Malerei, 2002, Directmedia
Publishing GmbH – *Wikimedia Commons*

The hero gazes at life, and sees his own image in the derelicts, *obsessives* [p. 124], sinners, criminals, of the twilights of *dawn* [p. 80] and *dusk* [p. 78]. He shies at his own fate presaged in that of the digging *skeletons* [p. 139]: he dreams his own end, embodied in terrifying *words* [p. 151]: 'The curtain had risen, and I was still waiting.' He is a *Midas* [p. 154], guided by an unknown Hermes, trapped into making gold from mud endlessly, then to achieve his freedom doomed to make iron from gold.

And in an ultimate piece of symbolism, Baudelaire, the poet, is *Icarus* [p. 166], flying on waxen wings made by his father Daedalus (creator of the artistic tradition) too near the sun, deceived in his pursuit of the Ideal, unable to accept mundane reality, his destroyed eyes searching the heavens, beneath the power of an unknown fire (mysterious Nature), lacking skill and strength, exceeding his capabilities, and ascending only to fall, as Icarus did, into the waves, the ocean of humanity, the sea of transience: doomed not to be able to name the abyss into which he falls (as Icarus gave his name to the Icarian Sea) since it is the Void, an abyss without names. Baudelaire's myths are the myths of failure and defeat, of those 'lost in this mean world, jostled by the crowd.' The hero ends not as hero, but as anonymous victim, drowned silently, buried by the weight of time and thwarted desire.

VII: TWILIGHT (THE VISION OF CALM)

I have argued that Baudelaire's art expresses the failures of relationship that became apparent in his age, and which taken together constitute the shift towards modernity. His own temperament and early history sensitised him to those aspects of life and his age, but his art embodies more than merely his own experience, it speaks for us all face to face with the real. These failures of relationship were new and profound. Baudelaire experienced them gradually as his own life expanded from the personal towards the social and then the universal.

Firstly the failure of the hyper-sensitive male in his relationship with Woman, precipitated by the polarised view of Woman inherited from religion and past society, but made doubly intense by his own struggles with his sexual impulse, his pride, and his jealousy. Polarity meant openness to the seductive power of sexuality, the concept of Woman as a sweet haven, but coupled it with longings for the Ideal, the paradise beyond the world. The result was an oscillation between dream and disgust, between intense alternatives, conflicting forces: it is represented by that curious rocking motion that pervades Baudelaire's thought and verse, and is symbolised by those tall vessels swaying in harbour between voyages, in a temporary and precious place of calm before voyage and tempest, before travel towards the Ideal, and shipwreck in the stormy waters of relationship.

Secondly there is the failure of relationship in religion, the failure of the illusion of deity, the loss of that harmonious and consoling Ideal, which is also a relationship with Woman, embodied in Christianity as the Virgin, or the Magdalene, Woman exalted or Woman fallen, Woman as ultimate forgiveness or Woman as the fount of evil ('simultaneously the sin and the Hell that punishes it.'). Baudelaire's dance with his gods, one of whom he calls Satan, is also his dance with Woman, and the one failure, the one tension, overlaps with the other. When the Ideal fails it fails in all its aspects: when one dimension of the Ideal fails it has a tendency to destroy all others, in the sensitive mind. Baudelaire is the heir to that erosion of religion by reason that the Enlightenment promoted, and the Revolution sealed. He inherits a French tradition of analysis and fearless thinking that could not leave him unscathed and that anticipated the continuing process in the intellectual life of our age, the retreat of religion as an intellectually acceptable answer in the face of science and analysis, the marginalisation of religion in advanced rights-based secular societies, and its relegation to the realms of the personal and private, as an emotional response to the problems of existence. God is dead, and there are no gods, but the longing, for many, remains.

Thirdly Baudelaire experienced the failure of relationship within society, its transformation due to the growing power of capitalism and trade, the rise of the cities, the loss of the Individual within the Crowd, the mass 'exile', defeat and subjugation of the weakest, the commoditisation of all aspects of human life which is again the trend that has extended through our own times, touching every corner of existence. Baudelaire, witnessing the powerful forces ranged against the Individual, the massive pressures to conform within the marketplace of commercialisation, understood how difficult the struggle against it would prove, felt in his own depths the pain of being in such a world, felt the death of the Romantic dream that it signalled, and coined the phrase 'the heroism of modern times.' The past is in conflict with the present, Romanticism with Modernity. Baudelaire embraces the ambiguities, the paradoxes, the antithetic forces, and by an effort of will creates classic art in the face of defeat. His own instincts are to see Woman polarised within heterosexual relationship, yet he celebrates Lesbianism, and the changing role of working class women at least in capitalist production. He despised progress, Americanisation, Brussels as a monument to commerce, 'the apotheosis of merchandising'. 'For the commercial man' he says, 'even honesty is a speculation for profit.' And yet he utilised in his poems the strange beauty of modern times, the tone and *frisson* of city landscapes, the dramas it created, the polarities it exhibited juxtaposed together, art and ugliness, poverty and wealth, law and crime, work and idleness, energy and exhaustion.

'L'Amante du Christ' – Félicien Rops (Belgian, 1833 – 1898)
LACMA Collections

Baudelaire is not a system-builder, not a consistent thinker: rather he is a witness, a powerful vessel of his times, experiencing, analysing, veering towards and away, a ship all at sea, on the great ocean of modernity. The Ideal society, perhaps Classical in Baudelaire's mind (though his utopias tend to be strange mineral worlds of light and distance, cold *landscapes* [p. 147], where Nature stilled, and shaped by art, produces calm within a dream) the Ideal society is lost or unachieved, and social disintegration, social chaos inhabits the interstices of what may seem social order. The Crowd, savage or dulled, submerges the Individual and brings isolation, indifference, defeat. The City, Paris, that Woman, 'the infamous Capital', fails the spirit, and destroys it, even as she *enchants* [p. 157].

Fourthly Baudelaire experiences a change in the relationship with Nature, traversed, mapped, and therefore no longer virgin. Her repetitions and boredoms have been explored, and there is nothing new there for the weary mind. Her resources are being plundered, and therefore her sacredness is less assured. While natural imagery pervades Baudelaire's verse, he tends towards the remote and non-human, stormy oceans, troubled woods, remote mountains, stars and suns, a Romantic extremism that is perhaps the last haven for his hopes and dreams, but an ambiguous haven, since Nature is too often the realm of transience, mortality and cruelty. Nature as the Goddess, is also Woman as an Ideal, and the failures of relationship with Nature, become failures of that Ideal also. She too betrays, causes ennui, turns away, disgusts. Yet she also calms and quietens. She is the cavern of resonance, echo, memory, symbol, reverberation, reflection. Her sunsets, her autumns, are ambiguous, her seas and skies are places of failure and shipwreck, yet they are also infinite regions where the spirit can free itself. Her eyes are wells of night and humiliation as well as suns, stars, beacons, bringers of beauty, a beauty that is also *sorrow* [p. 26]. In the ambiguity, in the ranging over extremes, Nature allows moments of peace and calm, as well as storms and drowning. Still, for Baudelaire, they are only moments, instants of peace, places offering hopes of new life, fragments of exhausted reflection or dream. They are temporary *harbours* [p. 82], the *twilights* [p. 161] that follow exertion and emotion, the havens of *memory* [p. 54], or the cool landscapes of *exhaustion* [p. 120] or *remote* [p. 12] reverie.

'La Pudeur de Sodome' – Félicien Rops (Belgian, 1833 – 1898)
LACMA Collections

Modernity offers us a struggle that seems doomed to failure. Yet Baudelaire's art is no failure. He proposed the only solution to the succession of days for the modern creative artist: work. He suggested the heroic mind-set necessary to swim in the ocean of the modern, that one should be 'a great man and a saint to *oneself*: that is the one vital thing': that 'true progress, that is to say moral progress, can occur only within the individual and by his own effort.' And he believed that 'genius is merely childhood rediscovered by an act of will,' while 'the child and the artist continually discover new themes in a single image.' 'We the poets and philosophers,' he cries, 'have redeemed our souls by ceaseless labour and by contemplation. By the constant exercise of our wills, and the lasting nobility of our devotion, we have created a garden of beauty for our use.'

Is there a way beyond Modernity, beyond the failures of relationship precipitated by older ways of seeing and knowing? Well, we cannot simply by-pass Modernity, or Baudelaire's vision. Aspects of that vision are real: aspects of the failure are true and deep. Modernity is still around us, with its failed religions, its commoditisation of human beings, its outdated polarities, and its destruction of the natural bond. We can only go beyond Modernity by addressing the failed relationships again in new ways, by establishing new relationships between men and women and between all human beings, new relationships with Nature and the Universe, new relationships between the Individual and society. We ourselves are witnesses to changing forms of those relationships whose failure Baudelaire experienced.

Firstly, the difficult revolution that allows Woman social justice, and frees her from the web of polarised thought that past ages and religions have cast about her, a revolution that also frees all disadvantaged human beings to take up their rightful places in society. That the Individual should no longer be objectified is the aim of such a revolution.

Secondly, the new, though often chilling, comprehension of our biological and social selves within the context of an intention-less universe devoid of gods and demons, open to exploration through the scientific method, a universe which, while still ultimately mysterious to us in its being and its organisation, is no longer some artefact of a strange deity, or the whim of a blind creator.

'Le Sphinx' – Félicien Rops (Belgian, 1833 – 1898)
LACMA Collections

Thirdly, a recognition of our relationship with the natural world, with the planet, in that difficult tension between achieving the means of our existence and freedom, while still preserving the un-violated essence of Nature, a relationship that ultimately must include an understanding of the sacredness of all life, and will confer rights on all our co-creatures, not least the right to as natural a life as possible, freed from abuse and exploitation, with Humanity taking its true place among the species.

Fourthly, the creation of new forms of society, which will curb the objectification and commoditisation of human beings, will return us to relationships of the spirit, and will reduce the significance of those of the process, or the object. Such societies do not yet exist except in embryo, but who is to say they are not possible in the future, perhaps on other planets than this one.

I am not suggesting that such changes of relationship solve all our problems, or remove the pains and torments of being human. Nor am I suggesting that Baudelaire was merely a child of his times, and that we somehow know better. Our relationships are changing, and while some aspects are repaired by that process, others are, or remain, damaged. I simply suggest that there are ways beyond Modernity that are not merely re-expressions of past failure in more refined, more abstruse or colder terms. Post-Modernism will give way to a New Realism, but not in the old sense of trying to replicate the world in art, rather in the fresh sense of seeking to understand our true place in the Universe, our true possibilities of communication and communion with each other, and the social forms that might best meet our greatest needs and aspirations.

That Baudelaire's work rings true for us, perhaps even more so than in his own age, indicates that he addressed permanent problems of relationship, that he expressed those deeply felt problems in poetry that satisfies and calms even as it challenges, and that we are still only beginning to address the new possibilities of relationship that might mitigate the problems he experienced: that there are, despite Baudelaire's vision, new worlds perhaps to create among the ruins of the old, new landscapes of the imagination to fashion. Let us allow Baudelaire, rightly, the last questioning word here:

'Those vows, those perfumes, those infinite kisses,

will they be reborn, from gulfs beyond soundings,

as the suns that are young again climb in the sky,

after they've passed through the deepest of drownings?

    - O vows! O perfumes! O infinite kisses!'

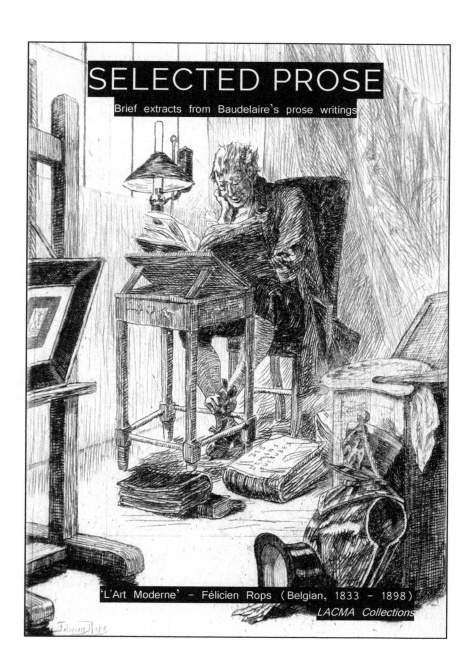

SELECTED PROSE

Brief extracts from Baudelaire's prose writings

'L'Art Moderne' – Félicien Rops (Belgian, 1833 – 1898)

LACMA Collections

I: FROM *LES PARADIS ARTIFICIELS* (*ARTIFICIAL PARADISES*)

From Moral. Hideous Nature, stripped of yesterday's radiance, resembles the melancholy debris of a banquet.

Balzac clearly thought that man's greatest disgrace and keenest suffering is the surrender of his will-power...the notion of letting his thoughts pass beyond his own control shocked him deeply.

He who has recourse to a poison in order to think will soon be unable to think *without* poison.

Magic makes dupes of them, shedding upon them a false happiness and an illusory light, whereas we, the poets and philosophers, have redeemed our souls, by unremitting toil and by contemplation.

II: FROM *LE PEINTRE DE LA VIE MODERNE* (*THE PAINTER OF MODERN LIFE*)

From III: Nevertheless genius is simply *childhood rediscovered* by an act of will.

So the lover of the life of the universe enters into the masses as into a huge reservoir of electrical energy.

From IV: Modernity is that which is ephemeral; fugitive, contingent on the occasion; it is half of art, whose other half is the eternal and unchanging.

From XI: Everything beautiful and noble is the result of reason and thought.

III: FROM *FUSÉES (ROCKETS)*

From I: What the Mind creates is more living than Matter.

From XI: Those great, resplendent ships, imperceptibly swaying (rocked) on these tranquil waters; those sturdy vessels with their air of idleness and nostalgia, surely they ask us in a mute language: 'When do we set sail for happiness?'

From XII: Hence it follows that irregularity, which is to say the unexpected, surprise, astonishment, is an essential part, and indeed the characteristic of beauty.

From XVI: I have discovered the definition of Beauty – of my Beauty. It is something ardent and sad, something a little vague, leaving room for conjecture.

From XVII: Inspiration always comes when a man *wishes*, but it does not always go when he wishes.

In certain almost supernatural states of the soul, the profundity of life is wholly revealed in the scene however mundane it may be that one has before one's eyes. It becomes Symbol.

From XVIII: Never despise a person's sensibility. Everyone's sensibility is their genius.

From XXII: I think the infinite and mysterious charm that lies in contemplating a ship, above all a ship in motion, is derived, in the first place, from its regularity and symmetry, which are among the primordial needs of the human spirit, and to the same extent as complexity and harmony; and in the latter case, of motion, to the continual generation and multiplication of all the imaginary curves and figures produced in space by the object's real elements.

The poetic idea which arises from this process of linear motion is the concept of some vast being, immense, complex, but rhythmic; a creature full of genius, suffering and sighing with every human ambition and sigh.

IV: FROM *MON COEUR MIS A NU*
(MY HEART LAID BARE)

From XII: A sense of solitude, from childhood. Despite my family, and above all among companions – the sense of an eternally lonely destiny.

From XV: Progress (that is to say, moral progress) can only be achieved within the individual, and by individual effort.

From XXXV: What is tedious about love-making is that it is a crime where one cannot do without an accomplice.

From XLIV: Fame is the result of the accommodation of a personality to the national foolishness.

From LII: To be a great man and a saint *to oneself*, that is the one important thing.

From LIX: Nomadic peoples, shepherds, hunters, farmers, even cannibals may be superior, because of their energy and personal dignity, to our Western races.

From LXV: It is this horror of solitude, this need to forget the *self* in another's flesh, that mankind so nobly terms *the need to love*.

From LXXI: To copulate is to aspire to enter into another – while the artist never emerges from the self.

From LXXIII: While still a child, I had two contrasting feelings in my heart, life's horror and life's ecstasy.

From LXXXI: Everything in this world sweats crime: the newspaper, the wall, the face of mankind.

From LXXXVIII: In the moral as in the physical, I have always sensed the abyss – not simply the abyss of sleep, but that of action, dream, memory, desire, regret, remorse, beauty, number....

I cultivated my hysteria with terror and delight. Now I suffer from a continual dizziness, and today, January 23rd 1862, I had a dire warning: – I felt the breath of the wing of imbecility pass over me.

From LXXXVIII: ...to consider this present moment as the most important of all moments....

From LXXXIX: No task is a long one but the task on which one dare not start.

V: FROM *THE BRUSSEL JOURNAL*

From IV: The child and the artist constantly find new themes in a single image.

From XXXIX: November 10th, 1864. Until I receive *proof* that in the real struggle (against Time) I am bound to be defeated, I will not allow myself to say I have made a failure of my life. All the same....

From XLIII: The re-creations of past ages are always false in this respect, that there is no life at their centre – everything has the same depth...

Prostitution is in essence a matter of lack of choice. Nevertheless the vocabulary and the aesthetic creed of prostitution always try to give the impression that choice is somehow present.

I like to imagine an art where the quality of permanence would be replaced by that of the provisional, an art constantly applied to life. Theatre; sunlight; dancers; and the dance.

Index of Poems by First Line

CHARLES BAUDELAIRE

Charles Baudelaire was born in Paris in 1821. His father died in 1827, his mother marrying Lieutenant-Colonel Jacques Aupick, the following year. The marriage appears to have had a significant influence on Baudelaire's emotional development, and attitude to women. He was educated at Lyon, and in Paris where he studied law, rejecting the career his step-father suggested in favour of literature. His stepfather however funded Baudelaire's voyage to Calcutta in 1841, touching at the island of Réunion south-east of Madagascar, ostensibly undertaken to allow him time to change his manner of life, but whose real legacy was the themes of ocean travel and exotic landscapes that permeate much of his poetry.

Squandering an inheritance, and mainly supported financially by his mother, he lived thereafter in Paris as a dandy and spendthrift. He was briefly involved in politics during the 1848 Revolution, but throughout the 1850's struggled with ill-health and financial debt while working on his seminal translations of Edgar Allan Poe and his major collection of poetry *Les Fleurs du mal*, published in 1857 the year of his step-father's death. He was also influential in the field of art criticism, championing the works of Delacroix, and as an essayist and commentator, credited with coining the term 'modernity' to mark the transformation of human life caused by the Enlightenment, the Revolution, and the industrialisation and increasing urbanisation of his day.

Dogged by illness and poverty, Baudelaire moved to Brussels in 1864, suffering a stroke followed by paralysis in 1866, and after hospitalization in Brussels he was transferred to Paris, dying there in August 1867.

About The Translator & Commentator

Anthony Kline lives in England. He graduated in Mathematics from the University of Manchester, and was Chief Information Officer (Systems Director) of a large UK Company, before dedicating himself to his literary work and interests. He was born in 1947. His work consists of translations of poetry; critical works, biographical history with poetry as a central theme; and his own original poetry. He has translated into English from Latin, Ancient Greek, Classical Chinese and the European languages. He also maintains a deep interest in developments in Mathematics and the Sciences.

He continues to write predominantly for the Internet, making all works available in download format, with an added focus on the rapidly developing area of electronic books. His most extensive works are complete translations of Ovid's Metamorphoses and Dante's Divine Comedy.

Made in the USA
Middletown, DE
15 May 2023

30626281R00146